Test Preparation Guide for LOMA 290

Insurance Company Operations

LOMA (Life Office Management Association, Inc.) is an international association founded in 1924. LOMA is committed to a business partnership with its worldwide members in the insurance and financial services industry to improve their management and operations through quality employee development, research, information sharing, and related products and services. Among LOMA's activities is the sponsorship of several self study education programs leading to professional designations. These programs include the Fellow, Life Management Institute (FLMI) program and the Fellow, Financial Services Institute (FFSI) program. For more information on all of LOMA's education programs, please visit www.loma.org.

Statement of Purpose: LOMA Educational Programs Testing and Designations

Examinations described in the *LOMA Education and Training Catalog* are designed solely to measure whether students have successfully completed the relevant assigned curriculum, and the attainment of any LOMA designation indicates only that all examinations in the given curriculum have been successfully completed. In no way shall a student's completion of a given LOMA course or attainment of a LOMA designation be construed to mean that LOMA in any way certifies that student's competence, training, or ability to perform any given task. LOMA's examinations are to be used solely for general educational purposes, and no other use of the examinations or programs is authorized or intended by LOMA. Furthermore, it is in no way the intention of the LOMA Curriculum and Examinations staff to describe the standard of appropriate conduct in any field of the insurance and financial services industry, and LOMA expressly repudiates any attempt to so use the curriculum and examinations. Any such assessment of student competence or industry standards of conduct should instead be based on independent professional inquiry and the advice of competent professional counsel.

Test Preparation Guide for LOMA 290

Insurance Company Operations

Information in this text may have been changed or updated since
its publication date. For current updates, visit www.loma.org.

LOMA Education and Training
Atlanta, Georgia
www.loma.org

PROJECT TEAM:

Authors:	Sean Schaeffer Gilley, FLMI, ACS, HIA, CEBS, AIAA, PAHM, MHP, AIRC, AAPA, ARA, FLHC
	Patsy Leeuwenburg, Ph.D., FLMI, ACS, FLHC, AIAA, ARA, AIRC, AAPA, PAHM
	Kelly W. Neeley, FLMI, ALHC, ACS, AIAA, PAHM
	Martha Parker, FLMI, ACS, ALHC, AIAA
Project Manager:	Julia K. Wooley, FLMI, ACS, ALHC, HIA, MHP
Production Manager:	Stephen J. Bollinger, ACS
Print Buyer:	Audrey H. Gregory, ACS
Typesetter:	Allison Ayers
Production Coordinator:	Amy Souwan
Technical Support:	David A. Lewis, FLMI, ACS
Administrative Support:	Marion Markus
Cover Design:	Kathleen Ryan, FLMI, FAHM, PCS, AIAA, AIRC, ARA

ISBN 1-57974-210-6

Printed in The United States of America

Contents

The TPG Companion CD-ROM now includes the practice questions and answers found in this booklet (along with answer choice explanations), and a sample exam also with answer choice explanations.

The TPG Companion CD-ROM is also the only place you will find the case studies for each chapter. For more information about the case studies, please turn to page 4.

Preface

Before You Begin...

Important Information on How to Study and Prepare for a LOMA Examination

Welcome to the Test Preparation Guide (TPG) for LOMA 290. This learning package was designed by LOMA to complement *Insurance Company Operations, Second Edition,* by Miriam A. Orsina, FLMI, PCS, ARA, PAHM, and Gene Stone, FLMI, ACS, CLU. Used along with the textbook, this TPG will help you master the course material as you prepare for the LOMA 290 examination. This TPG includes practice exam questions and a full-scale sample examination, both of which are provided in paper form as well as on an enclosed CD-ROM.

The nature of LOMA's self-study program offers two important benefits.

 First, you have the opportunity to learn important job-related information that will help you become a more knowledgeable and valuable employee.

 Second, a self-study program allows you to learn at your own pace and study at times that suit your own schedule.

You may need some help in developing the skills necessary for self study, or you may have some qualms about taking examinations. Even if you're very confident of your study skills, you need to understand what you will be expected to know once you have completed the course and how you can make sure you have mastered the course content. That's why LOMA developed the TPG.

Whether or not you are confident of your study skills and test-taking ability, you owe it to yourself to read through the next two sections in this manual. These introductory sections deal with the two issues mentioned above: effective studying and effective test taking. We've included many practical pointers that will help you study for and take the examination for this course. We have also explained how the TPG is designed and have given you advice on how to use it.

The remainder of the TPG is your guide to mastering the course material. By reading and working through this manual, you not only will discover how to focus your study, but you will also receive valuable practice in applying your knowledge and will be able to gauge your level of mastery of the material.

The TPG is your key to learning success.

Acknowledgments

The TPG for LOMA 290 was designed to provide a comprehensive self-directed learning approach to help students master the information in this course. As with all projects at LOMA, development of the TPG depended upon the combined efforts of many individuals.

Our thanks go to Julia K. Wooley, FLMI, ALHC, ACS, HIA, MHP, who acted as Project Manager, and to Carie W. Crane, FLMI, ACS, AIAA, ARA; Kristen L. Falk, FLMI, AAPA, ACS, AIAA, AIRC, ARA; Miriam A. Orsina, FLMI, PCS, ARA, PAHM; and Gene Stone, FLMI, ACS, CLU, for their valuable input and suggestions during the editing process. Thanks also go to Allison Ayers for her work typesetting this text and to Amy Souwan for her work coordinating the printing of the TPG and the production of the Interactive Study Aid CD-ROM. In addition, we thank Marion Markus for her administrative assistance.

Special thanks go to Ernest L. Martin, Ph.D., FLMI, who is the original author of the introductory material on becoming test-wise.

Sean Schaeffer Gilley, FLMI, ACS, HIA, CEBS, AIAA, PAHM,
MHP, AIRC, AAPA, ARA, FLHC
Patsy Leeuwenburg, Ph.D., FLMI, ACS, FLHC, AIAA,
ARA, AIRC, AAPA, PAHM
Kelly W. Neeley, FLMI, ALHC, ACS, AIAA, PAHM
Martha Parker, FLMI, ACS, ALHC, AIAA
Atlanta, Georgia
2005

Introduction

Study Tips

This section gives you practical advice on organizing and scheduling your study time so that you can master the assigned material for this course as efficiently and effectively as possible.

Getting Started

Before you begin the process of studying, take time to be sure that you have all the necessary "pieces," that you have evaluated all the resources available, and that you know where you're headed. Imagine finding out you have wasted your time by studying from the wrong edition of a text or for a test that has already been administered.

Materials and Resources

Assigned Text(s). Consult the current *LOMA Education and Training Catalog*[1] listing for this course to make sure you have all assigned texts. It will be essential to your success on the examination to read the assigned materials thoroughly. Check your text materials against the catalog listing for the academic year in which you plan to sit for the examination. If there have been multiple editions of assigned materials, be sure that you have the edition that will be used for testing purposes. In all cases, an edition change for a book used in a LOMA Insurance Education Program signals very substantial content changes. Students who study from previous editions of a text to prepare for an examination will be at a severe handicap when they sit for the examination. Although your company's Educational Representative or librarian may make every effort to maintain a current supply of textbooks for your use, it is your responsibility to secure the proper textbooks as you begin your study.

Recognize the value of the TPG as a companion to your textbook and use it. We designed the TPG to include features that have been shown to significantly improve examination pass rates for the students who use these aids.

Classes. Some companies offer classes to students. The regimen of preparing for classes is helpful to many students, and the chance to review material in a classroom setting reinforces learning. The effectiveness of your study efforts is likely to be enhanced if you use this TPG in combination with classes. LOMA studies have demonstrated the effectiveness of class attendance when it is combined with a study aid such as the TPG. Thus, if you have access to a class, you should participate. However, attending class is not a substitute for reading the assigned material and working through the TPG.

Examination Date. Check the current *LOMA Education and Training Catalog*[1] for the correct examination date for this course.

---

[1] The catalog is available from your LOMA Educational Representative or LOMA's Office of the Registrar. It is also available on LOMA's Web site at www.loma.org.

Preparing for the Examination

The amount of time you need to prepare for an examination depends on you—your comfort with the material and your comfort with your own study skills. Some people spend months studying; others spend a matter of days. We can't really advise you on the length of time you need to study because we don't know your experience with or schooling in the subject matter covered in this course, and we don't know your particular learning style. However, we can offer a few useful tips.

1. **Start early!** As soon as you enroll for the course, secure the assigned textual materials and begin planning your study schedule.

2. **Evaluate the material.** The examination for which you will sit is based exclusively on the assigned textual materials, ***including information in the body of the text and in the figures, tables, and insights in each chapter***. Read the textbook's preface and scan through each chapter in the book. Note the chapter objectives provided at the beginning of each chapter. Look at the Practice Questions and Sample Exam questions in the TPG. These steps should help you decide how easy or difficult the material seems to you and will help you plan your schedule. If you are not familiar with the material in a particular chapter, set aside time to go through the Case Studies for that chapter. The Case Studies are included on the Interactive Study Aid CD-ROM.

3. **Set study goals.** Determine how many days or weeks you have until your exam. Then look at the assigned texts and figure out how many chapters and pages are assigned. Next, use the chart on the following page to schedule your study time. Place a target date of completion in the appropriate box in the chart and check the column to the immediate right when study is completed. You might want to establish a schedule for reading the textual material and working through the TPG questions at a rate of one or two chapters per week. Another alternative would be to set a goal for completing your reading of the entire textbook and then to set goals for reviewing each chapter and completing all TPG questions. You decide. You should, however, keep two rules of thumb in mind: (1) If you spread your study over a long period, by the time you complete the last chapter, you may have forgotten what you studied at the very beginning of the course and will need to leave extra time for review, and (2) if you try to compress your studies into a very short period, you may not have time to read all the material and prepare for the examination. Some students find it useful to use motivational tools to help them stay on track and achieve their study goals. For example, you could find a fellow student and promise to check each other's progress, or you could plan to reward yourself for meeting certain study goals.

4. **Allow time to review.** Whether you tackle the material for this course one chapter at a time or all at once, you will need some time to review and organize what you have learned. The Case Studies, located on the Interactive Study Aid CD-ROM, help you learn the material presented in the text. The Practice Questions and Sample Exam in the TPG provide an excellent review of the text material and a measure of your understanding. The Practice Questions and Sample Exam also provide you with a preview of the types of questions you are likely to encounter when you take the actual exam.

A word of caution about reviewing for the examination for this course: Avoid relying on old examinations as study aids. The old tests you have may not be based on the currently assigned materials.

Study Schedule for LOMA 290

	Read Chapter	✓	Complete Case Studies	✓	Complete Practice Questions	✓
Chapter 1						
Chapter 2						
Chapter 3						
Chapter 4						
Chapter 5						
Chapter 6						
Chapter 7						
Chapter 8						
Chapter 9						
Chapter 10						
Chapter 11						
Chapter 12						
Chapter 13						
Chapter 14						
Chapter 15						
Chapter 16						
Chapter 17						
Chapter 18						
Take Sample Examination						

Using the TPG

Studying requires some methodical processes, but the results are worth the effort. Here is one process we recommend for learning the textual material and then preparing for the exam.

1.   **Read the learning objectives printed in the textbook or TPG.** The objectives let you know the relative importance of the subjects covered in the chapter. Keep these objectives in mind as you read the chapter material. Mastering each chapter's learning objectives will help you to be prepared to answer the questions on the examination.

2.   **Familiarize yourself with the chapter outline at the beginning of each chapter's practice questions in the TPG or in the text's Table of Contents.** Once you know your objectives, take a look at the framework the author has provided for your learning. The text contains an outline in the Table of Contents. The TPG contains a complete outline at the beginning of each chapter's Practice Questions. Notice the major headings in the outline—these are the broad subject areas covered in the chapter. Then look at the subheadings to see how the material fits together and what the important relationships within the chapter are. You may want to refer to the outline as you read and study, and you may also use it as a review aid when you've finished the chapter.

3.   **Read each textbook chapter at least once.** Some students prefer to read one chapter at a time, stopping to study and review the material using the steps outlined below. Others may wish to read the entire textbook through once before beginning to review and master the material. Choose the method that best suits you. As you read, be on the lookout for the topics, terms, and concepts that were mentioned in the objectives and outline. Use study techniques such as taking notes on a separate sheet, making notes in the margin of the book, and highlighting or underlining important material. *For the purposes of the examination, you are responsible for information in the body of the text and in the figures, tables, and insights that contain explanatory material in each chapter.*

4.   **Work through the Case Studies on the CD-ROM located on the inside back cover of this book.** Case Studies are designed to help you learn the material as you read through the text. Each Case Study covers material presented in one or more sections of the text by typically giving a situation and then asking questions about the situation. Several Case Studies are provided for each chapter of the text.

Students who are already very familiar with the material presented in a chapter may choose to skip the chapter's Case Studies and move on to the Practice Questions.

5.   **Answer the Practice Questions in the TPG or on the CD-ROM.** The TPG includes a set of Practice Questions for each chapter of the text. These questions are designed to enhance your test-taking ability by allowing you to practice answering the types of questions that appear on LOMA examinations. These questions may be based entirely on material from the chapter at hand, or they may build upon material from

preceding chapters. Do not assume that the number of Practice Questions for a given chapter is indicative of the chapter's relative weight on the examination itself.

The Practice Questions are presented in two formats. The first is the paper version, and an answer key with text references is located in the Answers to Practice Questions section. For each question you answer incorrectly, you should look up the correct answer in the textbook. The second version of the same Practice Questions is a computer software program found on a CD-ROM located on the inside back cover of the TPG. Students can use the software version of the Practice Questions as a study aid that provides an analysis of why each answer choice is correct or incorrect.

6. **Take the Sample Exam in the TPG or on the CD-ROM.** Actors have dress rehearsals, and students should too. The best way for you to determine if you are adequately prepared for a LOMA examination is to take the full-scale Sample Exam after you have read the textbook and worked the Practice Questions. The TPG includes one comprehensive examination similar in construction to an actual LOMA examination. This exam is presented in two formats. The first is a paper exam, and an answer key with text references is located in the Text References and Answers to Sample Exam section. The second version of the same Sample Exam is a computer software program found on a CD-ROM located on the inside back cover of this book. The software version of the Sample Exam can be used in two ways: (1) as a straight timed exam with your score furnished at the end or (2) as a study aid that provides analysis of the answer choices with explanations as to why each selection was correct or incorrect.

The Case Studies, the Practice Questions, and the Sample Exam were developed by staff members in LOMA's Examinations Department using LOMA examination guidelines.

7. **Adapt this process to your individual needs.** Use the techniques that have worked for you in the past and add the study suggestions from this list that you think will help you.

8. **Complete the student survey located at www.loma.org/surveys/stsurvey.htm.** The best way for us to be able to provide the best learning aids to students is to receive feedback from students. Please take a moment to fill out the survey so that we have an understanding of how well this guide helped prepare you for the exam.

Now that you have an understanding of how to plan your study time and how the TPG can assist you in mastering the assigned material, read the following section for tips on becoming "test-wise."

Becoming "Test-Wise"

If you are like most students taking LOMA examinations, you are not a full-time student and have not studied for or taken an exam in many years. Or you may never have taken an examination of the type that will be given for this LOMA program course. In either case, successful performance on a LOMA examination requires more than simply understanding the material; it requires understanding the examination process.

This section is designed to help you become "test-wise." First, we will acquaint you with the type of examinations LOMA administers. We will provide you with some strategies for taking an exam and we'll tell you how to avoid common test-taking mistakes. We'll give you a preview of the types of questions that you will see on LOMA examinations and show you how to use common sense and logic to enhance your chances of answering these questions correctly. And we'll tell you what to do *after* the examination (besides celebrate!).

Examination Structure and Administration

The examination for this LOMA course is offered in paper form twice per year. Students must be enrolled and fees paid well in advance of the scheduled examination administration date, and the examination administration schedule published in the *LOMA Education and Training Catalog* must be strictly adhered to. Students can receive an e-mail grade report approximately three to four weeks after the paper exam administration date. Students may also view exam results by logging into LOMANET and viewing their course history.

The examination for this course is also available on computer. I*STAR (Individually Scheduled Test and Results), LOMA's examination-by-computer system, is part of LOMANET, LOMA's Internet-based education system. The exam is also available at Prometric Testing Centers throughout the United States and Canada.

Students in the many companies that permit students to take I*STAR and/or Prometric exams enjoy the convenience of sitting for examinations at any time of the year, without regard to the strict administration schedule that governs paper examinations. I*STAR and Prometric students receive on-screen notification of examination results immediately upon completion of an examination.

You can enroll for a paper, an I*STAR, or a Prometric exam through LOMANET at www.lomanet.org. Your Educational Representative can inform you of your company's policies and procedures relating to paper, I*STAR, and Prometric exams.

The examination itself contains 75 questions and relies on a 100-point scoring system in which each question is worth $1^1/_3$ points. A passing score is 70.

What the Examination Will Cover

A test is a sample of knowledge. Limitations of space and testing time make it impossible to test every concept presented in the text materials. You can be certain, however, that the fundamental concepts of a course will be covered in every examination. LOMA emphasizes testing information that is both important and fair to the student.

The current emphasis of LOMA examinations is on putting the student in a decision-making role. In other words, students should be able to demonstrate that they are able to make functional use of the concepts learned. LOMA examinations require students not only to recognize facts or define terms, but also to apply concepts to situations and to draw conclusions. For example, instead of simply asking students to define the concept of net amount at risk, a LOMA examination may require students to calculate the net amount at risk for a particular life insurance policy.

Test-Taking Strategies

There is no substitute for adequate test preparation. Nevertheless, there are techniques that you can use to improve your chances of choosing the correct answer to examination questions and to avoid making test-taking mistakes.

1. **Read the entire question before attempting to answer it, and recognize the key concepts in the stem.** Each examination question contains critical pieces of information, or key concepts, and directions on how to use that information to select the correct answer. For example, a question might ask you for the definition of a term, for a characteristic of a particular product, or for a conclusion based on the "facts" of the situation. Once you have identified the key concepts, you can use them to evaluate the answer choices. The correct answer is the answer that incorporates all of the question's key concepts.

2. **Concentrate on those questions which you are absolutely or reasonably certain you know.** A sound practice in taking any examination is to focus on the questions you can answer confidently and leave until later those questions about which you have some doubt. Go through the entire examination once, answering the questions you can answer and skipping the questions you can't answer. Then go through the test a second time, providing answers to each of the questions you left blank.

3. **If you aren't sure which answer is correct, *make an educated guess*.** If you do not provide an answer to a question, it will automatically be marked incorrect; on the other hand, if you make an educated guess, you have at least a chance of being correct. You can generally use the process of elimination to narrow your choices and improve your chances of selecting the correct response. Start by going back to the key concepts you've identified for the question. If an answer choice does not address one or more of these key concepts, you can eliminate it as a possible response. Following this process almost always allows you to eliminate at least one answer choice. Quite often, the process leaves you with only one answer choice—the correct answer.

4. **Record your answers.** If you are taking a paper exam, record your responses on your answer sheet. Follow the instructions that appear on the examination cover page and on the answer sheet itself in marking your answers on the answer sheet. The answer sheets are graded by machine. If you are taking an electronic exam, record your answers by clicking the round button to the left of the answer choice or by pressing the corresponding number key on the computer keyboard.

5. **Go back through the test and check your answers.** Check the entries that you have recorded on your answer sheet (for a paper exam) or on the computer screen (for an electronic exam). Make sure that all questions have been answered and that your recorded answer choice matches your intended correct response for each question.

An Overview of Question Types Used in LOMA Exams

All of the questions used in LOMA examinations are multiple-choice questions which consist of two parts: (1) an introduction (called a "stem"), which includes key concepts related to the question topic and directions on how to use those key concepts; and (2) a list of possible answer choices. The student's objective is to select the answer choice that correctly satisfies the requirements of the stem.

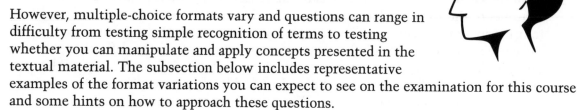

However, multiple-choice formats vary and questions can range in difficulty from testing simple recognition of terms to testing whether you can manipulate and apply concepts presented in the textual material. The subsection below includes representative examples of the format variations you can expect to see on the examination for this course and some hints on how to approach these questions.

Example 1: Straightforward Multiple-Choice Format

If the premiums for an employer-employee group life insurance contract are paid entirely by the employer, the group insurance plan is said to be

- (1) coinsured
- (2) vested
- (3) nonfunded
- (4) noncontributory

Most of the questions in a LOMA examination follow a straightforward multiple-choice format. In these questions, the question "stem" is followed by four answer choices, each of which consists of one term or fact that correctly completes the stem. The question in Example 1 asks for the term used to describe a particular type of insurance plan. The key concepts that will identify which of the four terms presented as answer choices is correct are (1) premiums, (2) employer-employee group life insurance, and (3) payments made solely by the employer. The correct answer is the response that correctly incorporates all of these key concepts. In Example 1, the correct answer is the term that describes a group insurance plan for which the employer pays 100% of the premium and the employees pay nothing.

If you are not sure which answer choice meets these requirements, you can narrow your choices by eliminating any answer choice you know is incorrect. For example, you can eliminate *coinsured* as a possible response because it has nothing to do with premiums. You can also eliminate *nonfunded* because it refers to pension plan funds rather than group life insurance.

Example 2: Multiple-Choice Column Format

Every insurance policy can be classified as being either a contract of indemnity or a valued contract. Dave Holmes is insured by an individual health insurance policy that provides him with basic hospital expense coverage; the policy will pay any hospital expenses Mr. Holmes may incur, subject to a maximum benefit of $300 per day. Mr. Holmes was recently hospitalized for 3 days, and the hospital charged $250 per day for his hospital stay. From the answer choices below, select the response that correctly classifies this insurance contract and that correctly identifies the total benefit amount payable to Mr. Holmes by his insurer in this situation.

	Type of contract	Benefit payable
(1)	valued contract	$750
(2)	valued contract	$900
(3)	contract of indemnity	$750
(4)	contract of indemnity	$900

Example 3: Multiple-Choice Series Format

Amos Reed entered into a contract with the Beacon Insurance Company to sell Beacon's life insurance products. With respect to the roles created by this agency contract, Mr. Reed is considered to be the

(1) principal, and Beacon is the agent
(2) agent, and Beacon is the customer
(3) service representative, and Beacon is the agent
(4) agent, and Beacon is the principal

Column format questions and series format questions require you to know more than one piece of information. As in straightforward multiple-choice questions, column format and series format questions present key concepts and instructions for answering the question. Example 2 instructs you to choose the answer that includes both the correct type of insurance contract and the correct benefit amount payable under the contract. Example 3 instructs you to choose the answer that identifies the roles assumed by an individual and an insurer in an agency relationship.

If you are unsure which answer is correct, or if you know only one piece of information, you can use the process of elimination to narrow the possibilities. For example, if you know that the benefit amount in Example 2 is $750 (3 × daily rate of $250) rather than $900 (3 × maximum benefit of $300), you can eliminate answer choices (2) and (4). You have only to determine whether the contract is a valued contract or a contract of indemnity. In Example 3, if you know that Mr. Reed is an agent, you can eliminate answer choices (1) and (3) and concentrate on determining whether Beacon is the customer or the principal. If you simply don't know, you at least have only two choices remaining from which to make an educated guess.

Example 4: Multiple-Choice "One Correct Statement" Format

The following statements are about the reinstatement of a fixed-premium life insurance policy. Select the answer choice that contains the correct statement.

(1) When such a policy is reinstated, the original policy is canceled and a new policy is issued.

(2) When such a policy is reinstated, the policyowner is charged a higher premium rate based on the insured's attained age.

(3) In most jurisdictions, when such a policy is reinstated, the contestable period expires and the insurer may not contest the policy for any reason.

(4) In order to reinstate such a policy, the policyowner is required to present satisfactory evidence of the insured's continued insurability and to pay all back premiums, plus interest.

This type of multiple-choice question presents a general topic and a series of statements related to that topic. The question stem identifies the topic and the criteria you are to use to evaluate the statements in the answer choices. In Example 4, the topic is reinstatement of a fixed-premium life insurance policy and you are directed to select the one correct statement.

Other questions might ask you to select the one **FALSE** statement in the series. There are no tricks in these questions, but they do require you to *read each answer choice carefully and completely* and to decide whether the answer choice is true or false.

You can narrow your choices on questions such as these by eliminating any answer choices that do not satisfy the criteria presented in the stem. In Example 4, you can safely eliminate all false statements. The more choices you eliminate, the greater your chances are of selecting the correct response.

Example 5: Multiple-Choice "Fill-In" Format

The paragraph below contains two pairs of terms enclosed in parentheses. Determine which term in each pair correctly completes the paragraph. Then select the answer choice containing the two terms that you have chosen.

The maximum annual contribution allowed under a Keogh plan is the **(lesser / greater)** of 25% of annual income or $30,000, and the owner of a Keogh plan **(can / cannot)** deduct this amount from his or her taxable income.

(1) lesser / can
(2) lesser / cannot
(3) greater / can
(4) greater / cannot

The two pieces of information you have to evaluate in this question are (1) the maximum annual contribution allowed under a Keogh plan and (2) the deductibility of plan contributions for Keogh plan owners. Perhaps you know that the maximum annual contribution allowed is the lesser of 25% of annual income or $30,000. This knowledge eliminates (3) and (4) as possible answer choices and increases your odds of answering correctly to 50 percent. All that remains is for you to determine whether the plan contributions are tax deductible.

Example 6: Multiple-Statement Format

The following statement(s) can correctly be made about societal changes in the United States that affect the annuities industry:

   A. The number of people entering retirement is decreasing.
   B. The average length of retirements is decreasing.

    (1) Both A and B
    (2) A only
    (3) B only
    (4) Neither A nor B

In order to answer this question, you have to evaluate *A* and *B* as statements about societal changes in the United States. Suppose you are uncertain about *A*, but you are certain that *B* is incorrect. In this case, you would be left with only (2) and (4) to consider, and your odds of guessing correctly would be 50 percent. To arrive at the correct answer, you need only consider whether *A* is a true statement.

Example 7: "Matching Questions" Format

Questions 18 and 19 are matching questions. Beside each question number is a description of a type of life insurance product. From the following answer choices, choose the term that correctly matches the description of each type of life insurance product.

    (1) Level term life insurance
    (2) Graded-premium whole life insurance
    (3) Continuous-premium whole life insurance
    (4) Limited-payment whole life insurance

18. Rex Larsen's life insurance policy provides a death benefit of $50,000 if his death occurs during the 15-year period in which the policy is in force. Mr. Larsen's annual premium payment remains the same throughout this 15-year period. At the end of the period, his coverage will expire.

19. Walter Fiermann will pay level premiums on his life insurance policy for 20 years. At the end of the 20-year period, Mr. Fiermann's policy will be paid up, but his coverage will continue throughout his life. His policy provides a death benefit of $100,000.

All of the multiple-choice formats discussed so far contain an introductory "stem" and a distinct set of answer choices. Matching questions consist of a description of the general topic under consideration and a set of instructions, followed by two or more questions and a single, common set of answer choices. Your objective is to select the answer choice that matches the term, statement, or situation presented in each question. Matching questions, as used in LOMA examinations, generally cover a relatively large amount of textual material and it is not uncommon for a series of matching questions to be drawn from thematically related material appearing in several textbook chapters. Usually, the number of answer choices exceeds the number of questions. Note, too, that more than four answer choices may be provided.

In order to arrive at the correct answer for matching questions, you should read the first question carefully and identify the key concepts. Then evaluate the answer choices according to the instructions provided in the stem and select the correct answer. Once you have completed the first question in the set, repeat the process for the next question. An important fact to remember about matching questions is that, **unless the directions for the series of matching questions specify otherwise, each answer choice is used only once.** This means that once you have identified the correct answer for one question, you can eliminate that answer choice when you evaluate the next question in the set.

Application Questions and Higher-Level Recognition Questions

As mentioned earlier, LOMA examinations may require students to demonstrate that they can make functional use of the concepts learned. Application questions ask you to manipulate information in such a way as to put into practice a concept that has been covered by the textual materials. In other words, application questions require you to put the knowledge you have gained to work in (1) predicting the consequences of a set of facts, (2) dealing with a real-life situation, or (3) solving a problem. Application questions, therefore, call for a higher level of conceptual skill than mere recognition of a concept, term, or formula.

Higher-level recognition questions do not require you to exercise the same level of question-answering skills that application questions require, but the knowledge required to answer these questions goes beyond basic concept recognition.

In order to highlight the differences between lower-level recognition questions, higher-level recognition questions, and application questions, consider examples 8 through 11.

Example 8: Lower-Level Recognition Question

The two major categories of life insurance products are term life insurance and permanent life insurance. *Permanent* life insurance is a form of insurance that

(1) provides coverage for the insured's lifetime
(2) provides coverage for a limited period of time specified in the policy
(3) pays regular benefits during the insured's entire lifetime
(4) pays benefits only if the insured is still alive at the end of the period specified in the policy

This question requires you merely to recognize one of the characteristics of permanent life insurance. It does not require you to manipulate any information or solve a problem.

Example 9: Higher-Level Recognition Question

Heather Friedman is covered by two group medical expense policies that provide identical benefits. Both policies contain the same deductible and coinsurance requirements. When Ms. Friedman was hospitalized for surgery, the policy designated as her primary plan paid benefits, but the policy designated as her secondary plan paid nothing, even though she filed claims under both policies. This information indicates that Ms. Friedman's secondary plan contains a

(1) split-dollar provision
(2) stop-loss provision
(3) partial disability benefits provision
(4) nonduplication of benefits provision

This question requires no manipulation of information—so it is not an application question—but it does require a higher level of recognition on your part than does Example 8. You not only have to know the definition of a nonduplication of benefits provision to answer this question correctly, but you have to be able to recognize the effect of such a provision in a real world example.

Example 10: Application Question

David Templeton was insured under a $100,000 whole life insurance policy. At the time of Mr. Templeton's death, the policy had a cash value of $10,000 and Mr. Templeton owed a total of $5,000 on an outstanding policy loan. The amount that is payable to the beneficiary of Mr. Templeton's policy is

(1) $90,000
(2) $95,000
(3) $100,000
(4) $105,000

This application item requires you to manipulate information and calculate a result based on that manipulation. A question of this type will present all of the data that you need to answer the question, and may even include some "red herring" data that does not bear on the correct answer but that might catch a student who hasn't studied.

All calculation questions (like example 10) are application items, but not all application items involve calculations. Consider, for example, the following question:

Example 11: Application Question

William Scott named his children, Trudy and Bob, as primary beneficiaries to share equally in the proceeds of an insurance policy on his life. He also named his wife, Marlene, as the policy's contingent beneficiary. When William died, Trudy and Marlene were the only surviving beneficiaries. In this situation, the death benefit will be paid

(1) entirely to Trudy
(2) entirely to Marlene
(3) to Trudy and Marlene in equal shares
(4) to Trudy and to Bob's estate in equal shares

This question asks you to predict an outcome based on a given set of facts and is, therefore, an application item.

Microcase-Based Questions

Most LOMA examinations contain at least one "microcase." Each microcase presents a fact situation and a series of questions that serve as the basis for more sustained testing of principles and a greater integration of concepts than you can get in a single question. The microcase fact situation may be presented in one or two short paragraphs, or it may take up half a page or more. Typically, the questions included in the microcase are application or higher-level recognition items.

Examination writers at LOMA attempt to achieve two objectives in every microcase: (1) verisimilitude, or the semblance of actuality, and (2) cross-chapter integration, or the incorporation of concepts from various sections of the textbook on which the examination is based. Microcases, therefore, provide you with the opportunity to bring a number of concepts and a fairly broad spectrum of knowledge to bear on a more realistic situation than can be encountered in a single question.

For example, a microcase might present a person who owns an individual medical expense insurance policy. The microcase situation might provide information on the policy's deductible, coinsurance percentage, and coordination of benefits (COB) provision, and inform you of various medical expenses incurred for various procedures. All of this information in the microcase situation could lead to a series of questions that would require you to know (1) the type of deductible included in the policy, (2) the amount of benefits payable by the insurer, (3) the amount of expenses paid by the insured, (4) whether the insured is eligible for benefits for a type of procedure, and so on.

Even a short microcase situation can provide a foundation for asking a large number of questions that require you to thoroughly understand the underlying concepts and apply those concepts in a complex situation.

As with the increased use of application questions and higher-level recognition items (which we noted above), the use of microcases is an indication that your studies should go beyond the mere memorization of the definitions of key terms and concepts.

Some Test-Taking Myths

No matter how diligently you prepare for the examination, you will be handicapped if you adhere to some test-taking myths that circulate through groups of students with almost self-perpetuating force. Here are a few.

Myth 1: **Answer choice (1) is the best choice if it is necessary to guess the correct answer to a question because examination writers usually place the correct answer first.**

Fact: The distribution of correct answers to the questions appearing on a LOMA examination is fairly evenly balanced among the available answer choices.

Myth 2: **There is usually a pattern to the answer key responses.**

Fact: There is no pattern to the order of the correct responses to the questions in a LOMA examination except that the distribution of correct responses is evenly balanced, or relatively so.

Myth 3: **Always choose the longest response to a question because examination writers are careful to qualify the correct answer more than they qualify the incorrect answers.**

Fact: Because the examination writers at LOMA are especially alert to this tendency in examinations in some other testing programs, they take special care to avoid such a pattern. Short answers or average-length answers are just as likely as long answers to be correct.

After the Examination

Paper Examinations

You will not be permitted to take your copy of the examination booklet with you when you leave the examination room. However, the proctor is authorized to return your copy of the examination booklet to you after 24 hours have elapsed. Putting your name on the front of your examination booklet will ensure that you receive the same copy you had while sitting for the examination. If you recorded your selected answers in your examination booklet, you can further reinforce the knowledge that you have gained by looking up the correct answers in the textbook. Contact your Ed Rep to obtain a copy of the text references for the examination. You can also view and download text references at LOMA's Web site at www.loma.org.

Occasionally, students may wish to challenge the validity of certain questions. The basis for such challenges varies; it may be a perception that a question is not clearly worded, or that the correct answer does not accurately reflect the textual passage on which it is based, or that the textual passage is at variance with current practices in the insurance industry. Infrequently, a typographical error may be cited as the basis for a challenge.

If you believe that there is good reason to challenge a test question after you have taken the test, put your challenge in writing and forward it to your Ed Rep, who will forward it to the LOMA Education Division for consideration. Receipt of your challenge will be acknowledged by return mail. Be sure to submit any challenges so that they are received by the date specified in the Education Catalog. Any resulting changes can then be taken into account before answer sheets are scored.

The important point to keep in mind about such challenges is that each one is investigated by the professional staff in the LOMA Education and Training Division. If the staff committee doing the investigation finds that there is merit to the challenge—and the benefit of the doubt is always given to the student—that committee will recommend that the answer key be changed to give credit for more than one answer choice. The effect of such a recommendation is to give the students who chose the allowable responses credit for the challenged questions, regardless of whether the intended correct answer was chosen.

As an additional step, the LOMA Education and Training Division creates various statistical reports designed to call to the staff's attention any irregularities in response patterns to questions. Each such irregularity is investigated in detail to ensure that the reason for it is not some erroneous component of the question. If such an irregularity does lead to discovery of an error in a question, multiple answers will be allowed.

Once final grades are posted, it is not possible to make any changes in them.

I*STAR and Prometric Examinations

Administrative regulations pertaining to electronic examinations do not permit students to keep a record of their answer responses or transport any materials out of the testing room. Exam proctors at I*STAR and Prometric testing facilities are required to collect all notes, scratch paper, etc., from students. These regulations are intended to enhance the security of an examination series available throughout the year.

I*STAR and Prometric students, however, may still avail themselves of the opportunity to challenge test questions. A student who believes that a test question is erroneous should record the question number and convey the challenge immediately to the Ed Rep, who will forward it to LOMA. I*STAR and Prometric examination results are subject to the same extensive statistical checks as are paper examination results.

Case Studies and Practice Questions

NEW!

Case Studies for each chapter are now available.

The Case Studies are included on the CD-ROM located on the inside back cover of this book. Please see page 4 for more details about the Case Studies.

The Practice Questions are now presented in two formats.

The first is the paper version, and an answer key with text references is located in the Answers to Practice Questions section. The second version of the same Practice Questions is a computer software program on a CD-ROM located on the inside back cover of this book. Answer choice explanations are available on the CD-ROM.

Life Insurance Company Operations

Chapter Objectives

After studying this chapter, you should be able to

- Describe the different types of financial institutions that comprise the financial services industry

- Describe the roles that life insurance companies play in the financial services industry

- List the essential operations that all life insurance companies undertake

- Explain the concepts of risk and risk management

- Explain the purpose of strategic planning for life insurance companies

- Explain how insurers use strategic alliances and outsourcing as part of strategic planning for operations

Outline of Major Topics

The Roles of Life Insurance Companies
    Providers of Financial Security
    Financial Intermediaries
Life Insurance Company Operations
    Integration Among Functional Areas
Risk Management in Life Insurance Companies
Strategic Planning for Operations
    Strategic Alliances
    Outsourcing

Case Studies

The case studies for this chapter are on the CD-ROM located on the inside back cover of this book. Please see page 4 for more details about the Case Studies.

Practice Questions

1. Under one type of life insurance product, the death benefit is payable only if the insured dies during the period specified in the policy. This type of life insurance product is known, by definition, as

    (1) term life insurance
    (2) endowment life insurance
    (3) variable life insurance
    (4) cash value life insurance

2. The paragraph below contains two pairs of terms enclosed in parentheses. Determine which term in each pair correctly completes the paragraph. Then select the answer choice containing the two terms that you have chosen.

    Annuities can be classified in several different ways. An annuity that provides periodic income payments that generally are scheduled to begin one annuity period after the date on which the policy is purchased is known as **(a deferred / an immediate)** annuity. Under a **(fixed / variable)** annuity, the amount of the policy's accumulated value and/or the amount of the periodic income payments fluctuate in accordance with the performance of one or more specified investment funds.

    (1) a deferred / fixed
    (2) a deferred / variable
    (3) an immediate / fixed
    (4) an immediate / variable

3. A depository institution is a type of financial institution that specializes in accepting deposits and making loans. In the United States, examples of depository institutions include

    A. Commercial banks
    B. Savings and loan associations (S&Ls)
    C. Insurance companies
    D. Credit unions

        (1) A, B, C, and D
        (2) A, B, and C only
        (3) A, B, and D only
        (4) A and B only
        (5) C and D only

4. One functional area of a typical life insurer is comprised of actuaries. The actuarial staff of a typical insurer is primarily responsible for

   (1) managing the company's investments according to the guidelines established by the company's management
   (2) maintaining the financial records of each of the company's businesses, preparing reports on the company's financial condition, and filing required financial statements with appropriate regulatory bodies
   (3) ensuring that the company conducts its operations on a mathematically sound basis, assisting with pricing and product development, and calculating policy reserves and policy dividend amounts
   (4) ensuring that the company classifies proposed life insureds so that their mortality experience, as a group, falls within the range of the mortality rates assumed at the time of product design and pricing

5. The Memorial Insurance Company recently discovered that a flaw in its claim fraud detection system allowed certain fraudulent claims to go undetected. Because the company has mistakenly paid these fraudulent claims, its operating costs increased significantly. In order to combat this situation, Memorial provided claim analysts with additional training and established a new claim fraud detection system, which it will monitor closely. It is correct to say that the type of risk Memorial faced in this situation is known as

   (1) operational risk
   (2) liquidity risk
   (3) market risk
   (4) credit risk

6. Life insurance companies sometimes develop strategic alliances to strengthen their competitive positions and provide new opportunities for growth. Insurance industry strategic alliances usually take one of two legal forms: a partnership or a joint venture. With regard to these two forms of strategic alliance, it is correct to say that a

   (1) partnership usually is limited to one project with a specified duration
   (2) partnership is a contract between two or more parties that agree to pool their funds and talents and share in the profit and loss of the enterprise
   (3) joint venture usually is a permanent relationship that can be the basis of many projects
   (4) joint venture is the practice of hiring an external vendor to perform specified operations

Answers to Practice Questions begin on page 95.
Answer choice explanations are available on the CD-ROM on the inside back cover of this book.

2 Competition, Regulation, and Ethics in the Life Insurance Industry

Chapter Objectives

After studying this chapter, you should be able to

■ Describe the impact of the Gramm-Leach-Bliley Act on the operations of U.S. life insurance companies

■ Describe how commercial banks, securities firms, and mutual fund companies compete with life insurance companies for insurance product sales

■ Describe the life insurance regulatory system in the United States

■ Identify the three general areas of solvency regulation and describe how these areas are regulated

■ Discuss the importance of ethics in the life insurance industry

■ Explain how insurers can improve the ethical decision making and professionalism of their employees and insurance producers

Outline of Major Topics

Competition in the Life Insurance Industry
  Recent Reforms in the U.S. Financial Services Industry
  Sources of Competition for Insurance Product Sales
Regulation of the Life Insurance Industry
  Insurance Regulators
  Areas of Insurance Regulation
Ethics for Life Insurance Companies
  The Importance of Ethics
  Improving Ethics in the Life Insurance Industry

Case Studies

The case studies for this chapter are on the CD-ROM located on the inside back cover of this book.

Practice Questions

1. The paragraph below contains two pairs of terms enclosed in parentheses. Determine which term in each pair correctly completes the paragraph. Then select the answer choice containing the two terms that you have chosen.

   The competitive environment in the United States financial services industry changed considerably in 1999 with the passage of the federal **(Gramm-Leach-Bliley Act / USA PATRIOT Act)**. This law **(permits / prohibits)** banks, insurance companies, and broker/dealers to affiliate in a holding company structure.

   (1) Gramm-Leach-Bliley Act / permits
   (2) Gramm-Leach-Bliley Act / prohibits
   (3) USA PATRIOT Act / permits
   (4) USA PATRIOT Act / prohibits

2. The Summit Bank, a commercial bank in the United States, wishes to distribute life insurance products as an agent of the Manatee Insurance Company. Summit wants to distribute these products to bank customers through its branches. Assuming that Summit does not operate in the states of Connecticut, Massachusetts, or New York, it most likely is correct to say that Summit

   (1) is prohibited by law from selling Manatee's insurance products to bank customers
   (2) may sell Manatee's insurance products to bank customers, and Summit is required to assume the risk on any such insurance sold
   (3) may sell Manatee's insurance products to bank customers, but Summit cannot assume the risk on any such insurance sold
   (4) can sell only savings bank life insurance (SBLI) products to bank customers

3. The laws that specifically regulate an insurer's capitalization, product design, and policy reserves to ensure that the company is financially able to meet its debts and pay policy benefits when they come due are known, by definition, as

   (1) directives
   (2) model laws
   (3) solvency laws
   (4) market conduct laws

4. The paragraph below contains two pairs of terms enclosed in parentheses. Determine which term in each pair correctly completes the paragraph. Then select the answer choice containing the two terms that you have chosen.

    Governments are the primary regulators of the life insurance industry. In the United States, the primary authority to regulate the insurance industry rests with the **(state governments / federal government)**. The federal law which specifically granted this right is the **(Employee Retirement Income Security Act (ERISA) / McCarran-Ferguson Act)**.

    (1) state governments / Employee Retirement Income Security Act (ERISA)
    (2) state governments / McCarran-Ferguson Act
    (3) federal government / Employee Retirement Income Security Act (ERISA)
    (4) federal government / McCarran-Ferguson Act

5. In the United States, insurance laws and regulations are influenced by a nongovernmental organization which fosters uniformity in state regulation and cooperation among state insurance departments by developing model laws and regulations. This organization, which has no regulatory authority by itself, is known as the

    (1) Securities and Exchange Commission (SEC)
    (2) International Association of Insurance Supervisors (IAIS)
    (3) Insurance Regulatory and Development Authority (IRDA)
    (4) National Association of Insurance Commissioners (NAIC)

6. In most countries, regulations designed to protect the solvency of insurance companies focus on three basic categories: assets, liabilities, and capital and surplus. For an insurer, *investments* are the most important element in the category of

    (1) assets, which are things the company *owns*
    (2) assets, which are amounts the company *owes*
    (3) liabilities, which are things the company *owns*
    (4) liabilities, which are amounts the company *owes*

7. In Canada, the nongovernmental committee of provincial insurance regulators that looks at emerging industry and business trends and works toward harmonizing legislation through model codes and standardized reporting requirements is known as the

    (1) Chartered Insurance Institute
    (2) Canadian Council of Insurance Regulators (CCIR)
    (3) Office of the Superintendent of Financial Institutions (OSFI)
    (4) Organization for Economic Cooperation and Development (OECD)

8. The Aberman Insurance Company, a United States company, operates in a state which has a law patterned after the National Association of Insurance Commissioners (NAIC) Life Insurance Disclosure Model Regulation. Therefore, Aberman provides all of its prospective policyowners with a publication that explains how to determine how much life insurance coverage they need, describes the various types of life insurance policies, and educates consumers about how to compare the costs of similar types of policies. This publication is known, by definition, as

    (1) a prospectus
    (2) a policy form
    (3) a Buyer's Guide
    (4) an Annual Statement

9. In the United States, many of the states have enacted privacy laws modeled after the NAIC Insurance Information and Privacy Protection Model Act (Model Privacy Act). This Act establishes standards for the collection, use, and disclosure of information gathered in connection with insurance transactions, such as underwriting and claim evaluation. State laws based on the NAIC Model Privacy Act apply to insurance purchased for

    (1) both personal needs and for business or professional needs
    (2) personal needs, but not to insurance purchased for business or professional needs
    (3) business or professional needs, but not to insurance purchased for personal needs
    (4) neither personal needs nor for business or professional needs

10. For this question, if answer choices (1) through (3) are all correct, select answer choice (4). Otherwise, select the one correct answer choice.

    The major self-regulatory market conduct initiative in the North American insurance industry is the Insurance Marketplace Standards Association (IMSA). IMSA is a voluntary association of United States and Canadian life insurers that have qualified for membership by undergoing a comprehensive assessment of their market conduct. The steps that a life insurer must take to qualify for IMSA membership include

    (1) adopting IMSA's Six Principles of Ethical Market Conduct
    (2) adopting IMSA's Code of Life Insurance Ethical Market Conduct
    (3) satisfying the requirements of IMSA's assessment program, which examines the company's operations
    (4) all of the above

Answers to Practice Questions begin on page 95.
Answer choice explanations are available on the CD-ROM on the inside back cover of this book.

CHAPTER 3

Life Insurance Company Formation and Restructuring

Chapter Objectives

After studying this chapter, you should be able to

■ Discuss the procedures for incorporating and licensing a life insurance company

■ Describe the differences between a stock insurance company and a mutual insurance company

■ List the benefits and challenges of mergers and acquisitions

■ Explain why many insurers are part of holding company systems

■ Discuss the advantages and disadvantages of demutualization

■ Describe the steps involved in the process of demutualization

■ Describe the effects of a mutual holding company conversion on a mutual insurer and its policyowners

Outline of Major Topics

The Corporate Structure of Life Insurance Companies
Requirements for Incorporation
    Incorporating in the United States
Insurance Company Licensing
    Licensing of Life Insurance Companies in the United States
Stock and Mutual Life Insurance Companies
    Proportion of Stock Companies to Mutual Companies
    Participating and Nonparticipating Life Insurance Policies
Changing the Corporate Structure
    Mergers and Acquisitions
    Holding Company Systems
    Demutualization
    Mutual Holding Company Conversion

Case Studies

The case studies for this chapter are on the CD-ROM located on the inside back cover of this book.

Practice Questions

1. Insurance laws in the United States require that life insurers organize and operate as corporations. One characteristic of a corporation is that the

    (1) corporation is not a distinct legal entity
    (2) corporation cannot be a party in a legal action
    (3) corporation continues beyond the death of any or all of its owners
    (4) corporation's owners are personally liable for the debts of the corporation

2. The following statements are about the incorporation of an insurance company in the United States. Select the answer choice containing the correct statement.

    (1) An insurance company must incorporate in every state in which it does business.
    (2) Once established, a corporation's certificate of incorporation cannot be revoked, even if the corporation violates conditions included in its articles of incorporation.
    (3) If an application for incorporation is filed with a state administrative agency rather than with the state insurance department, the incorporation of the new insurance business does *not* need to be approved by the state insurance commissioner.
    (4) Before granting an insurer the right to operate as a corporation, state insurance officials investigate the moral character of each of the company's organizers, the company's business plan and financial projections, and the company's plans of organization and operations.

3. In the United States, the document that grants a corporation its legal existence and its right to operate as a corporation is known, by definition, as the

    (1) articles of incorporation, and it is issued by the state government
    (2) articles of incorporation, and it is issued by the federal government
    (3) certificate of incorporation, and it is issued by the state government
    (4) certificate of incorporation, and it is issued by the federal government

4. Consider the following insurance companies with regard to their location of incorporation:

    • The Able Insurance Company, a United States company, is incorporated in State A.
    • The Benevolent Insurance Company, a United States company, is incorporated in State B.
    • The Crimson Insurance Company is incorporated in Canada.

    From the point of view of *State A*, it is correct to say that

    (1) Able and Benevolent are both domestic insurers, and Crimson is a foreign insurer
    (2) Able is a domestic insurer, and Benevolent and Crimson are both foreign insurers
    (3) Able is a domestic insurer, and Benevolent and Crimson are both alien insurers
    (4) Able is a domestic insurer, Benevolent is a foreign insurer, and Crimson is an alien insurer

5. Consider the following United States companies:

    - The Houston Life Insurance Company, which is organized as a stock company that pays stockholder dividends
    - The Bennet Mutual Insurance Company, which is organized as a mutual company

    The following statements are about these two companies. Select the answer choice containing the correct statement.

    (1) Houston's stockholders are owners of the company and as such, they are involved in the company's day-to-day operations.
    (2) Houston's preferred stockholders are paid their dividends before any dividends can be paid to the company's common stockholders.
    (3) The people that own insurance policies issued by Bennet most likely have policy rights, but they do not have membership rights.
    (4) As a mutual company, Bennet is better able to gain access to capital sources necessary for growth and expansion than is Houston.

6. John Campbell owns a life insurance policy issued by the Granite Mutual Insurance Company. Mr. Campbell's policy is classified as a participating policy. As the owner of a participating policy, Mr. Campbell most likely has the right to

    (1) share in the insurance company's divisible surplus by receiving a policy dividend, which is considered a return of part of the premium Mr. Campbell paid for the insurance policy
    (2) receive a portion of the insurance company's net profits through the distribution of periodic stock dividends
    (3) receive a guarantee that any dividends paid to him will be of a fixed amount
    (4) vote in elections of the company's board of directors on the basis of one vote per $1,000 of insurance owned

7. The Northern Mutual Insurance Company and the View Bank entered into a transaction wherein the assets and liabilities of the two companies were combined. As a result, the View Bank ceased to exist as a separate entity, and Northern Mutual became the Northern Financial Services Company. In this situation, it is correct to say that Northern Mutual and View Bank changed their corporate structure through the type of transaction known as

    (1) a merger, and Northern Financial Services must be a stock company
    (2) a merger, and Northern Financial Services must be a mutual company
    (3) an acquisition, and Northern Financial Services must be a stock company
    (4) an acquisition, and Northern Financial Services must be a mutual company

8. When the Live Insurance Company and the Oak Insurance Company combined to form one company, the Live Oak Insurance Company, they achieved *economies of scale*. This information indicates that, as a combined company, Live Oak most likely was able to

   (1) improve the persistency rates of insurance policies issued by the former companies
   (2) reduce the company's unit costs as the size of its operations increased
   (3) increase the company's unit costs as the size of its operations increased
   (4) achieve greater short-term profitability by avoiding expenses related to integrating the people, processes, and systems of the former companies

9. The Shelby Life Insurance Company created the Kilkenny Holding Company. Kilkenny controls Shelby and also owns and controls other subsidiaries. This information indicates that Kilkenny is the type of holding company known as

   (1) an amalgamation holding company
   (2) a due diligence holding company
   (3) a downstream holding company
   (4) an upstream holding company

10. In the United States, a mutual insurer can restructure its organizational form in one of two general ways: demutualization or conversion to a mutual holding company. With regard to these two methods of corporate restructuring, it generally is correct to say that, compared to demutualization, conversion to a mutual holding company

   (1) is less costly
   (2) takes longer to accomplish
   (3) enables the insurer to raise more capital in public markets
   (4) has less flexibility in regard to the timing of an initial public offering (IPO) of stock

Answers to Practice Questions begin on page 95.
Answer choice explanations are available on the CD-ROM on the inside back cover of this book.

CHAPTER 4

The Organizational Structure of Insurance Companies

Chapter Objectives

After studying this chapter, you should be able to

■ Describe the basic activities in each functional area of a typical life insurance company

■ List four ways in which an effective organizational structure benefits a company

■ Explain the kinds of information that are contained in an organization chart

■ Compare the duties and responsibilities of a company's board of directors, officers, managers, and supervisors

■ State the differences between insurance companies that are organized by function, product, territory, and profit center

■ Discuss alternative configurations to the traditional organizational pyramid

■ Explain the role that committees play in a company's operations

Outline of Major Topics

Functional Areas in a Life Insurance Company
Marketing
Actuarial
Underwriting
Customer Service
Claim Administration
Annuity Administration
Investments
Accounting
Information Technology
Legal Operations
Compliance
Human Resources
Other Common Functional Areas

Components of the Organizational Structure
> The Organization Chart
> Pyramidal Structure and Levels of Authority
> Centralized and Decentralized Organizations
> Line Units and Staff Units

Traditional Ways Insurers Organize Work Activities
> Organization by Function
> Organization by Product
> Organization by Territory
> Organization by Profit Center or Strategic Business Unit

Alternative Organizational Shapes

Committees

Case Studies

The case studies for this chapter are on the CD-ROM located on the inside back cover of this book.

Practice Questions

1. The responsibilities of the marketing area in a life insurance company typically include

    A. Conducting research to identify the company's target customers and their needs
    B. Conducting research to identify competitors' new products and new product features
    C. Working with other departments in the company to develop new products and to revise current products as customer needs, economic conditions, and regulatory requirements change
    D. Establishing and supporting distribution systems for the company's products
    E. Preparing advertising campaigns and promotional materials

    > (1) A, B, C, D, and E
    > (2) A, B, and E only
    > (3) A, C, and E only
    > (4) A and D only
    > (5) B and C only

2. One functional area in a life insurance company is the underwriting area. The underwriting department typically has the responsibility for all of the following activities **EXCEPT**

    > (1) making sure the company accepts only those life insurance applicants whose actual mortality rates, as a group, do not exceed the mortality rates assumed when the premium rates for a particular product were calculated
    > (2) evaluating and classifying proposed insureds according to the guidelines established for each product
    > (3) participating in the negotiation of reinsurance agreements
    > (4) handling reinsurance administration

3.   An effective organizational structure benefits a company by providing a means of establishing authority, delegation, responsibility, and accountability. An organizational structure in which employees are answerable for how well they use their right to make decisions and take action and for how effectively they carry out their assigned tasks and duties benefits a company by establishing

     (1) authority
     (2) delegation
     (3) responsibility
     (4) accountability

4.   An insurer's formal internal organization can be exhibited in a visual display of the various job positions in the company and the formal lines of authority and reporting among employees. This visual display is known as

     (1) an organization chart
     (2) an operational plan
     (3) a staff unit
     (4) a line unit

5.   The paragraph below contains two pairs of terms enclosed in parentheses. Determine which term in each pair correctly completes the paragraph. Then select the answer choice containing the two terms that you have chosen.

According to the principle of **(unity of command / enterprise risk management (ERM))**, each employee within an organization should be under the authority of only one person and be accountable to only that person. In today's organizational environment, insurance companies typically **(can / cannot)** adhere strictly to this principle.

     (1) unity of command / can
     (2) unity of command / cannot
     (3) enterprise risk management (ERM) / can
     (4) enterprise risk management (ERM) / cannot

6.   In the traditional pyramidal structure of an organization, the top level of an insurer's organization chart typically shows the company's

     (1) president
     (2) stockholders
     (3) policyowners
     (4) board of directors

7. Management at the Aqua Insurance Company is responsible for the company's strategic and tactical planning activities. Aqua has each of the following levels within its chain of command:

    - A chief executive officer (CEO)
    - A chief operating officer (COO)
    - A vice president for each major division
    - Several middle-level managers in charge of departments within divisions

    Within Aqua's chain of command, the level of management that is most involved in *tactical* planning and least involved in strategic planning is the

    (1) CEO level
    (2) COO level
    (3) vice president level
    (4) middle management level

8. The organizational structure of a business can be described as having characteristics of centralization or decentralization. Compared to a decentralized organization, a *centralized* organization typically tends to

    (1) have greater administrative costs
    (2) have more consistent company policies and actions
    (3) allow managers to respond more quickly to situations
    (4) delegate more decision-making authority to middle- and lower-level managers

9. From the answer choices below, select the terms that correctly complete blanks **A**, **B**, and **C** in the following paragraph.

    Three important types of authority in an organization are line authority, staff authority, and functional authority. __**A**__ authority is authority held by staff unit personnel to advise or make recommendations to line unit personnel. __**B**__ authority is direct authority over workers, and it corresponds directly to the organization's chain of command. __**C**__ authority is a staff unit member's formal or legitimate authority over line units in matters related to the staff member's area of expertise.

	A	**B**	**C**
(1)	Line	Staff	Functional
(2)	Staff	Line	Functional
(3)	Functional	Staff	Line
(4)	Functional	Line	Staff

10. At the Cadence Insurance Company, work is distributed according to the company's lines of business. A major division of the company administers each line of business and handles most of the functional activities for that line of business only. However, the company makes decisions regarding the divisions' operations and provides resources to support those operations. A few functions, such as investments, legal, accounting, compliance, and human resources, are handled through centrally administered departments. This information indicates that Cadence uses an organizational structure known as organization by

     (1) profit center
     (2) function
     (3) territory
     (4) product

11. The Gardner Insurance Company uses an organizational structure that consists of three basic layers. The top layer contains executives who are responsible for formulating Gardner's strategic plan. The middle layer consists of a smaller group of middle managers who coordinate the functions of the bottom layer, which typically consists of a large and diverse group of technical/professional employees. At Gardner, the middle managers are generalists, rather than functional specialists. With regard to organizational structure, Gardner correctly can be classified as

     (1) a network organization
     (2) a cluster organization
     (3) an hourglass organization
     (4) a traditional pyramid organization

12. The Holly Insurance Company formed a permanent committee made up of key executives and several members of the company's board of directors. This committee meets quarterly to set policy for the company's accounting department, review all company policies and the internal audit plan, oversee internal and external financial and market conduct audits, and review the company's periodic financial statements. This committee, which provides continuing advice to Holly's executives, is an example of the type of committee known as

     (1) a task force
     (2) a project team
     (3) a standing committee
     (4) an ad hoc committee

Answers to Practice Questions begin on page 95.
Answer choice explanations are available on the CD-ROM on the inside back cover of this book.

CHAPTER 5

Marketing Activities and Strategies

Chapter Objectives

After studying this chapter, you should be able to

- ■ Describe the basic marketing activities of a life insurance company

- ■ List the four variables that comprise the marketing mix

- ■ Explain the terms *market segmentation* and *target marketing*

- ■ Describe the three main sources of marketing information

- ■ List the factors from a life insurance company's internal environment and external environment that affect the insurer's marketing operations

- ■ Describe the function of a marketing plan

- ■ Explain why many insurers have decided to expand their operations internationally

Outline of Major Topics

The Marketing Mix
Positioning
Market Identification
    Market Segmentation
    Target Marketing
Matching Products to Target Markets
Marketing Information
    Internal Marketing Environment
    External Marketing Environment
The Marketing Plan
    Developing the Marketing Plan
    Elements of the Marketing Plan
    Communicating the Marketing Plan
    Control and the Marketing Plan
Marketing Strategies for Company Growth
    International Expansion

Case Studies

The case studies for this chapter are on the CD-ROM located on the inside back cover of this book.

Practice Questions

1. The paragraph below contains two pairs of terms enclosed in parentheses. Determine which term in each pair correctly completes the paragraph. Then select the answer choice containing the two terms that you have chosen.

   Organizations can be classified as product-driven or market-driven. A **(product-driven / market-driven)** insurer first determines the needs of the customers who make up the life insurance and annuity markets and then develops products, services, and distribution methods to satisfy those needs. Most life insurance companies today are **(product-driven / market-driven)**.

   (1) product-driven / product-driven
   (2) product-driven / market-driven
   (3) market-driven / product-driven
   (4) market-driven / market-driven

2. Marketers develop specific strategies for planning and controlling each of four primary marketing variables—price, promotion, product, and distribution—collectively known as the marketing mix. With regard to the definitions of these four variables in the context of the marketing mix, it is correct to say that the term

   (1) *price* refers to the goods, services, or ideas that a seller offers to customers to satisfy a need
   (2) *promotion* refers to the collection of activities that a seller uses to influence customers to purchase and distributors to sell a product
   (3) *product* refers to the activities and resources involved in making products available to customers
   (4) *distribution* refers to the monetary value of whatever customers give in exchange for the product being marketed

3. The paragraph below contains two pairs of terms enclosed in parentheses. Determine which term in each pair correctly completes the paragraph. Then select the answer choice containing the two terms that you have chosen.

   (Market segmentation / Target marketing) is the process of dividing large, heterogeneous markets into smaller, more homogeneous submarkets that have relatively similar needs. One such submarket for insurance products is the **(organizational / consumer)** market, which consists of individuals who buy insurance products and services for personal or family use.

   (1) Market segmentation / organizational
   (2) Market segmentation / consumer
   (3) Target marketing / organizational
   (4) Target marketing / consumer

4. The Garrett Life Insurance Company attempts to satisfy the needs of different segments of the total life insurance market by offering a number of products and marketing mixes designed to appeal to the different segments of that total market. This information indicates that Garrett is using the target marketing strategy known as

    (1) mass marketing
    (2) concentrated marketing
    (3) differentiated marketing
    (4) undifferentiated marketing

5. An insurer's marketing environment consists of all the elements in the company's internal and external environments that directly or indirectly affect the company's ability to carry out its marketing activities. An example of a factor found in an insurer's *internal* environment is

    (1) the rate of unemployment
    (2) an insurer's size and financial resources
    (3) an increase in the level of interest rates
    (4) the ongoing evolution of technology

6. One characteristic of a typical marketing plan for an insurer is that it

    (1) spells out the marketing aspects of an insurer's strategic plans and provides details about the company's marketing mix
    (2) includes a careful review of the insurer's short-range business objectives, but not its long-range business objectives
    (3) affects the insurer's marketing department only
    (4) covers a time period of five to ten years

7. Marketing plans differ from company to company, depending on the size of the company and its marketing objectives. But most marketing plans include the following elements: an executive summary, a situation analysis, marketing objectives, marketing strategies, tactical/action programs, budgets, and evaluation and control methodology. The element of the marketing plan known as a *situation analysis* is best described as

    (1) an evaluation of the internal and external environmental factors that affect the insurer's marketing operations
    (2) a summary of the plan's proposed actions, the costs associated with those actions, and the intended results of those actions
    (3) a description of the marketing activities that are to be performed, the people who are responsible for performing the activities, and the results that are expected to be produced by the activities
    (4) a schedule of projected expenses and revenues that shows how funds will be allocated to various elements of the marketing mix and how funds will be divided among the activities associated with each element

8. The following statements are about international expansion of insurers. Select the answer choice containing the correct statement.

   (1) An insurer considering international expansion typically does not need to be concerned about regulatory requirements in the potential new market, because the insurer is only subject to the regulatory requirements of the country in which it is based.

   (2) For a multinational corporation, the foreign country in which the multinational corporation does business is known as that company's home country.

   (3) International expansion typically increases the adverse effect that an economic downturn in any one country will have on the insurer's overall financial performance.

   (4) International expansion enables an insurer to diversify its operations and its risks, which generally has a positive effect on the company's financial position.

Answers to Practice Questions begin on page 95.
Answer choice explanations are available on the CD-ROM on the inside back cover of this book.

CHAPTER 6

Product Development

Chapter Objectives

After studying this chapter, you should be able to

- List the five main steps in the product development process

- Explain how insurance companies gather and screen ideas for new products

- Describe how insurers conduct a comprehensive business analysis of a product idea

- Identify the functional areas that are involved in technical design and describe the role of each area in this aspect of product development

- Describe the main activities involved in product implementation

- Discuss how and why insurers monitor early sales of a new product

Outline of Major Topics

Personnel Involved in Product Development
    Product Development Teams
The Product Development Process
    Product Planning
    Comprehensive Business Analysis
    Technical Design
    Product Implementation
    Sales Monitoring and Process Review
The Importance of Effective Product Development

Case Studies

The case studies for this chapter are on the CD-ROM located on the inside back cover of this book.

Practice Questions

1. For a particular insurer, a *new product* may be

    A. A product never before issued to the public by any insurer
    B. A product previously offered by competitors, but not by the insurer
    C. A revision of a product currently offered by the insurer

    (1) A, B, and C
    (2) A and B only
    (3) A and C only
    (4) B and C only

2. The Cannon Life Insurance Company assigned both a project sponsor and a project manager to oversee and manage the new product development process. Amanda Seabolt is the project manager for Cannon's product development unit. As a project manager, Ms. Seabolt most likely is responsible for

    (1) giving written approval to the completion of each step in the product development process
    (2) serving as the project's advocate at the senior management level
    (3) controlling the day-to-day aspects of the project
    (4) approving changes to the scope of the project

3. One phase of the product development process involves quickly evaluating new product ideas to identify the ideas that warrant further investigation. This quick evaluation of new product ideas is known, by definition, as

    (1) test marketing
    (2) idea screening
    (3) idea generation
    (4) initial business planning

4. One element of a comprehensive business analysis is a feasibility study. During a feasibility study, an insurer's product development team typically

    (1) studies all of the environmental factors that might affect sales of a product
    (2) conducts research designed to determine the operational and technical viability of producing and offering the product and the impact of the new product on the company's existing products
    (3) specifies the product's basic characteristics, the manner in which the benefits will be provided, applicable fees and charges, and any limitations on issuing policies
    (4) estimates the product's financial requirements, potential unit sales, revenues, costs, and profits

5. The following statements are about policy filing in Canada and in the United States. Select the answer choice containing the correct statement.

    (1) In Canada, insurers must file policy forms with provincial insurance regulators in only two instances: to obtain a license to sell insurance products in the province and to offer a variable life insurance product.
    (2) In the United States, variable insurance contracts and the sales materials to be used with them must be filed with and approved by both the state regulatory authorities and the National Association of Insurance Commissioners (NAIC).
    (3) In the United States, an insurer is not obligated to obtain approval of a product's policy form from the state insurance department prior to selling the product in the state.
    (4) Policy filing typically takes place before the technical design phase of new product development.

6. Many states in the United States have laws patterned after the National Association of Insurance Commissioners (NAIC) Life Insurance Illustrations Model Regulation, which seeks to protect consumers and promote customer education by providing life insurance illustration formats, standards for use, and disclosure requirements. The Model Regulation defines an illustration as a presentation or depiction that includes

    (1) all guaranteed and nonguaranteed elements of a life insurance policy
    (2) only guaranteed elements of a life insurance policy
    (3) only nonguaranteed elements of a life insurance policy
    (4) all nonguaranteed elements of a life insurance policy, and some guaranteed elements of a life insurance policy

Answers to Practice Questions begin on page 95.
Answer choice explanations are available on the CD-ROM on the inside back cover of this book.

CHAPTER 7

Pricing Insurance Products

Chapter Objectives

After studying this chapter, you should be able to

- Identify three types of pricing strategies used by insurers

- Describe the three most important components of pricing for life insurance and life annuities: investment earnings, cost of benefits, and the loading charge

- Discuss the function and behavior of mortality rates in pricing for life insurance and life annuity products

- Interpret data from a mortality table and calculate the number living from one age to the next

- Describe the characteristics of mortality data and different types of mortality tables

- List some examples of acquisition expenses, development expenses, maintenance expenses, and overhead expenses for insurance products

- Explain the difference between gross premiums and net premiums for life insurance

- Explain the purpose of asset-share models and the importance of the break-even point and the break-even period in an asset-share model

- Discuss how insurers manage the results of the pricing process

Outline of Major Topics

Setting Pricing Objectives and Strategies
Making Assumptions for Pricing
  Investment Earnings and Interest Rates
  Cost of Benefits and the Mortality Factor
  The Loading Charge
Bundled and Unbundled Pricing
  Bundled Pricing for Life Insurance
  Bundled Pricing for Annuities
Policy Reserves and Cash Values
Profit-Testing Actuarial Assumptions
Managing Pricing Results
  Favorable Deviations
  Adverse Deviations

Case Studies

The case studies for this chapter are on the CD-ROM located on the inside back cover of this book.

Practice Questions

1. One of the first steps that insurance company actuaries take in pricing a new life insurance product is to establish a pricing objective for the product. The purpose of this pricing objective is to

    (1) measure the product's proposed pricing structure against several profitability standards
    (2) specify what the company wants to achieve with the product's pricing
    (3) determine the amount customers must pay for each unit of coverage under the new product
    (4) describe how the company will use the product's financial features as a variable in the marketing mix

2. The following statements are about the investment earnings element used in pricing insurance products that have an investment component. Select the answer choice containing the correct statement.

    (1) According to the time-value-of-money concept, the value of a sum of money earning interest generally is less in the present than it will be in the future.
    (2) The investment earnings element used in pricing is equal to the total value of the investment at the end of a specified period minus the principal amount invested.
    (3) If all other factors remain constant, an increase in either the interest rate or the amount of time an investment is left to grow at interest will result in a decrease in the value of the investment.
    (4) Investment earnings typically have a greater impact on short-term products than on long-term products.

3. Roger Atwood, an insurance company actuary, is entering actuarial assumptions into a product model to establish the pricing for a new insurance product. One of these assumptions is the value of the product's *cost of benefits*, which is equal to the insurer's

    (1) total potential benefit obligations to customers
    (2) total potential benefit obligations to customers multiplied by the expected probability that each benefit will be payable
    (3) actual benefit obligations to customers plus the company's operating and investment expenses for the product
    (4) actual benefit obligations to customers minus the company's operating and investment expenses for the product

4. Mortality rates affect the cost of benefits for life insurance and life annuities in the payout period. In general, as the mortality rate increases, the cost of benefits

    (1) increases for both life insurance and life annuities in the payout period
    (2) increases for life insurance, but decreases for life annuities in the payout period
    (3) decreases for life insurance, but increases for life annuities in the payout period
    (4) decreases for both life insurance and life annuities in the payout period

5. Insurance company actuaries typically base the mortality assumptions used in pricing life insurance and annuity products on statistics presented in various mortality tables. By definition, a basic mortality table is a type of mortality table that

    (1) is used for calculating policy reserves
    (2) shows for each age a single set of mortality rates for both males and females
    (3) includes projected mortality rates for a population consisting of life insureds only
    (4) has no safety margin built into the mortality rates

6. An actuary for the Hartwell Insurance Company used information from a mortality table to determine the mortality rates for the following individuals:

    • Jason Bentley, age 22
    • Elizabeth Fargo, age 32
    • George Karas, age 42
    • Barbara Lovett, age 42

    If the mortality rates for these individuals are based only on age and sex, then the individual who has the highest mortality rate is

    (1) Mr. Bentley
    (2) Ms. Fargo
    (3) Mr. Karas
    (4) Ms. Lovett

7. One purpose of including a loading charge in an insurance product's pricing structure is to cover the insurer's operating expenses. An insurer's operating expenses include all of the following expenses **EXCEPT** those associated with

    (1) keeping policies in force
    (2) the cost of benefits
    (3) developing new products
    (4) obtaining and issuing new business

8. The loading included in a product's pricing structure not only helps defray the insurer's operating expenses, but also compensates the insurer for policy lapses. A *policy lapse* occurs when a

    (1) policyowner fails to pay sufficient premiums during a specified period
    (2) policy terminates because of the death of the insured
    (3) policy reaches maturity
    (4) policy expires while the policyowner is still alive

9. Pricing structures can be classified as bundled pricing structures or unbundled pricing structures. The pricing structure of a deferred annuity usually is

    (1) *bundled* during both the accumulation period and the payout period
    (2) *bundled* during the accumulation period and *unbundled* during the payout period
    (3) *unbundled* during the accumulation period and *bundled* during the payout period
    (4) *unbundled* during both the accumulation period and the payout period

10. Insurance regulation generally requires insurers to maintain at least a minimum amount of policy reserves for all in-force policies. The following statements are about these required reserves. Select the answer choice containing the correct statement.

    (1) Policy reserve calculations typically include a loading charge.
    (2) The policy reserve for an insurance product usually is smaller than the cash value for the same product.
    (3) Policy reserves represent actuarially adjusted values of future contractual benefits and future gross premiums.
    (4) To provide greater protection against risks, insurers typically base policy reserve valuations on actuarial assumptions that are less favorable to the insurer than the expected values.

11. Before finalizing the pricing of a new life insurance product, an actuary for the Granite Insurance Company tested the product's profitability by entering various sets of assumptions for the product's investment returns, mortality, and expenses into an asset-share model. One set of assumptions produced the following possible values:

End of Year	Asset share per $1,000 of initial premium	Reserve per $1,000 of initial premium	Surplus per $1,000 of initial premium
5	$1,280	$1,310	– $30
6	$1,361	$1,374	– $13
7	$1,445	$1,439	$ 6
8	$1,538	$1,503	$35

According to this scenario, Granite's new product is expected to begin making a profit during year

(1) 5
(2) 6
(3) 7
(4) 8

12. Insurance companies typically build safety margins into their product pricing structures to protect themselves against unfavorable contingencies and adverse deviations. An adverse deviation is defined as an unexpected condition in which a product's

(1) actual profitability is lower than its assumed profitability
(2) assumed profitability is lower than its expected profitability
(3) actual exposure to risk is lower than its assumed exposure to risk
(4) assumed exposure to risk is lower than its expected exposure to risk

Answers to Practice Questions begin on page 95.
Answer choice explanations are available on the CD-ROM on the inside back cover of this book.

CHAPTER 8

Product Distribution

Chapter Objectives

After studying this chapter, you should be able to

■ Describe the steps in the sales process for insurance products

■ Differentiate among personal selling distribution systems, financial institutions distribution systems, and direct response distribution systems

■ Explain how agency-building distribution systems differ from nonagency-building distribution systems and describe the various types of agency-building and nonagency-building distribution systems

■ Explain how variable products are distributed in the United States

■ Describe the strategies that banks use to market insurance products

■ Describe the primary types of media used in direct response distribution systems

■ Describe the activities involved in direct response distribution

■ Discuss some of the important factors that insurance companies consider when determining which product distribution system or systems to use

Outline of Major Topics

Distribution Systems
Personal Selling Distribution Systems
    The Sales Process
    Agency-Building Distribution Systems
    Nonagency-Building Distribution Systems
Financial Institutions Distribution Systems
    Broker/Dealers
    Banks
    Insurance Companies
Direct Response Distribution Systems
    Direct Response Distribution Activities
Distribution Channel Decisions
    Characteristics of Customers in Target Markets
    Characteristics of the Products the Company Sells

Costs Associated with Each System

Degree of Control the Insurer Intends to Exercise over Distribution

Characteristics of the Insurer

Insurer's External Marketing Environment

Case Studies

The case studies for this chapter are on the CD-ROM located on the inside back cover of this book.

Practice Questions

1. The paragraph below contains two pairs of terms enclosed in parentheses. Determine which term in each pair correctly completes the paragraph. Then select the answer choice containing the two terms that you have chosen.

    Insurance producers working in personal selling distribution systems typically enter into an agency relationship with at least one insurance company. Under the terms of this relationship, the producer is considered to be the **(agent / principal)** and has the authority to solicit applications for insurance policies and to collect **(initial / renewal)** premiums for those policies.

    (1) agent / initial
    (2) agent / renewal
    (3) principal / initial
    (4) principal / renewal

2. Needs analysis is the step in the insurance sales process in which an insurance producer

    (1) identifies, locates, and contacts potential insurance customers
    (2) develops a detailed picture of a customer's personal and financial situation
    (3) describes recommended products to a customer to stimulate the customer's interest and motivate the customer to make a purchase
    (4) answers a customer's questions and objections and persuades the customer to submit an application for a recommended product

3. In the United States, agents working in a career agency distribution system can be either exclusive agents or agent-brokers. One characteristic of an *agent-broker* is that the agent-broker is

    (1) considered to be an insurance company employee
    (2) not under contract to any particular insurance company
    (3) permitted to place business with more than one insurer
    (4) exempt from state insurance licensing requirements

4. The following statements describe types of personal selling distribution systems. Select the answer choice containing an example of a general agency distribution system.

    (1) The Cheshire Insurance Company uses a distribution system that is designed to generate consumer-initiated sales at an insurance facility, such as an office or information kiosk, located in a store or other establishment at which consumers conduct personal business.

    (2) The Diligent Insurance Company uses a field office that is established and maintained by an independent businessperson who is under contract to Diligent and whose primary function is to build and manage an office of full-time career agents focused on distributing Diligent's products within a defined territory.

    (3) The Epigram Insurance Company uses exclusive agents to solicit applications, collect initial and renewal premiums, and provide service for policies sold to lower-income households in specified geographic areas or territories.

    (4) The Fremont Insurance Company uses group representatives to sell and service group insurance products to businesses and other organizations.

5. One indication of the insurance industry's movement from a product-driven orientation to a market-driven orientation is the increased use of cross-selling. By definition, cross-selling is the process of

    (1) identifying a customer's needs for additional products when selling a primary product
    (2) retaining in-force insurance or annuity policies
    (3) persuading a prospect to purchase a recommended insurance product
    (4) telephoning or visiting an insurance prospect with whom a producer has had no prior contact

6. The Lively Insurance Company markets individual and group insurance products to various employer-employee groups through worksite marketing arrangements. One advantage of these worksite marketing arrangements is that they allow

    (1) Lively to eliminate distribution and administration costs for the products it sells to employees
    (2) Lively to collect policy premiums directly from participating employees
    (3) policyowners to retain ownership of insurance coverage purchased through a worksite marketing plan even if they are no longer employed by the employer that sponsored the plan
    (4) employers to offer their employees products that can be used instead of existing employee benefit programs

7. The Omega Insurance Company is considering distributing its products through either a brokerage distribution system or a personal-producing general agency system. The primary difference between these two systems is that

    (1) brokers are allowed to sell only Omega's products, whereas personal-producing general agents (PPGAs) can place business with several insurers

    (2) brokers generally must meet minimum production requirements, whereas PPGAs generally are not subject to production requirements

    (3) brokerage systems are agency-building distribution systems, whereas personal-producing general agency systems are nonagency-building distribution systems

    (4) broker contracts resemble career agents' contracts, whereas PPGA contracts resemble general agents' contracts

8. The following statements are about the sale of variable life insurance and variable annuity products in the United States. Select the answer choice containing the correct statement.

    (1) Unlike ordinary life insurance and annuity products, variable life insurance and variable annuity products are regulated at the federal rather than the state level.

    (2) To sell variable life insurance or variable annuity products, a person or firm must be registered with the Securities and Exchange Commission (SEC) as a broker/dealer.

    (3) Variable life insurance and variable annuity products are not subject to any special regulatory requirements and can be distributed through any type of distribution system.

    (4) An insurance company can market variable life insurance and variable annuity products only if the insurer is a subsidiary of a registered broker/dealer.

9. The Ashcroft Bank distributes life insurance and annuity products to its customers through platform employees. By definition, platform employees are

    (1) employees of an independent general agency that operate out of office space provided by the bank

    (2) full-time commissioned insurance producers who operate out of their own offices outside the bank

    (3) bank employees who are trained and licensed to sell insurance products

    (4) salaried insurance company employees who are specifically trained in the techniques of marketing and servicing insurance products through banks

10. Life insurance companies typically distribute their products through one of three general types of distribution systems: personal selling distribution systems, financial institutions distribution systems, and direct response distribution systems. One characteristic of a direct response distribution system is that it

    (1) relies exclusively on direct mail to deliver an insurer's sales offer or advertising message

    (2) allows customers to purchase products directly from the insurer, without face-to-face contact with a sales representative

    (3) is used by relatively few insurance companies

    (4) has historically been best suited for complex products that require extensive explanation

Answers to Practice Questions begin on page 95.
Answer choice explanations are available on the CD-ROM on the inside back cover of this book.

9 Home Office Support for Distribution Systems

Chapter Objectives

After studying this chapter, you should be able to

- Explain how the home office supports agency-building distribution systems in recruiting, training, licensing, and compensating producers

- Describe the types of sales support and technology support that insurance companies may provide to agency-building distribution systems

- Describe the activities that insurance companies conduct to monitor the market conduct of their producers

- Discuss the similarities and differences between the home office's support for agency-building distribution systems and for nonagency-building distribution systems

- Describe how the home office supports the broker/dealers and banks that distribute the company's products

Outline of Major Topics

Case Studies

The case studies for this chapter are on the CD-ROM located on the inside back cover of this book.

Practice Questions

1. The success of an insurance company's product distribution activities depends in great part on the performance of its salespeople, so insurers and agency managers continually seek new insurance producers. The primary responsibility of agency managers in this process is to

    (1) oversee insurance producer licensing
    (2) enter into contracts with qualified insurance producers
    (3) set the compensation and benefit levels for new insurance producers
    (4) recruit promising insurance producers

2. In response to the Gramm-Leach-Bliley (GLB) Act in the United States, State A and State B enacted reciprocity requirements related to the licensing of insurance producers. This information indicates that

    (1) State A and State B enacted licensing laws that are basically the same
    (2) State A and State B agreed to give residents of the other state certain privileges, on condition that the other state grant residents of their state the same privileges
    (3) an insurance producer who sells products in both State A and State B must be licensed by either State A or State B, but not both
    (4) the specific qualifications necessary to obtain a producer's license do not vary from State A to State B

3. For this question, if answer choices (1) through (3) are all correct, select answer choice (4). Otherwise, select the one correct answer choice.

    In order to sell insurance products in the United States, insurance producers must be licensed. The requirements a producer must satisfy in order to obtain an insurance producer's license include

    (1) submitting a completed application and paying a licensing fee to the appropriate regulatory body
    (2) passing a written examination in all lines of insurance
    (3) filing with the insurance regulatory authority a written notice of appointment made by an officer of an insurance company
    (4) all of the above

4. The commission schedules used by three insurance companies (Company X, Company Y, and Company Z) to compensate producers for sales of life insurance policies are listed below.

Policy Year	Company X	Company Y	Company Z
1	50%	15%	30%
2	5%	15%	15%
3	5%	15%	10%
4	5%	15%	10%

From the answer choices below, select the response that correctly identifies the type of commission schedule used by each company.

Company X	Company Y	Company Z
(1) heaped schedule	levelized schedule	level schedule
(2) levelized schedule	level schedule	heaped schedule
(3) level schedule	heaped schedule	asset-based schedule
(4) heaped schedule	level schedule	levelized schedule

5. For this question, if answer choices (1) through (3) are all correct, select answer choice (4). Otherwise, select the one correct answer choice.

Insurance companies in the United States are subject to a variety of regulatory requirements regarding the use of sales materials. These regulatory requirements apply to

  (1) product brochures developed by the company's home office
  (2) insurance illustrations developed by producers for use during presentations to customers
  (3) advertisements that promote an idea, a philosophy, a company, or an industry
  (4) all of the above

6. The Harmony Insurance Company distributes information such as forms, product updates, sales illustrations, notices of rate changes, and policy transaction summaries through its extranet. Information on Harmony's *extranet* most likely is accessible to

  (1) Harmony employees and to selected external parties
  (2) Harmony employees only
  (3) selected external parties only
  (4) all external parties, without restrictions

7. Insurance companies provide support to producers whether they distribute products through agency-building distribution systems or nonagency-building distribution systems. Compared to career agents in agency-building distribution systems, independent producers in nonagency-building distribution systems generally

  (1) receive more services from the home office
  (2) earn higher commission rates on sales
  (3) are subject to greater home-office control over day-to-day activities
  (4) have more contact with the insurer

8. Four insurance marketing strategies often used in bank distribution channels are third-party marketer (TPM) strategies, platform employee strategies, insurance agency strategies, and promotion/lead generation strategies. The amount and type of support that an insurance company provides for a bank distribution channel varies according to which marketing strategy the bank uses. From the answer choices below, select the response that correctly identifies a strategy that most likely requires a high level of service from the insurer's home office and a strategy that most likely requires a low level of service from the insurer's home office.

	High level of service	Low level of service
(1)	TPM strategy	promotion/lead generation strategy
(2)	platform employee strategy	insurance agency strategy
(3)	insurance agency strategy	TPM strategy
(4)	promotion/lead generation strategy	platform employee strategy

Answers to Practice Questions begin on page 95.
Answer choice explanations are available on the CD-ROM on the inside back cover of this book.

CHAPTER 10 Life Insurance Underwriting

Chapter Objectives

After studying this chapter, you should be able to

- Identify the key participants in life insurance underwriting and explain the role of each type of participant

- List the four general risk classes to which life insurance underwriters assign proposed insureds

- Discuss the medical, personal, and financial risk factors that life insurance underwriters evaluate for individual proposed insureds

- Explain how group life insurance underwriting differs from individual life insurance underwriting

- Identify the activities involved in field underwriting and in home office underwriting for individual life insurance applications

- Explain the typical information contained in Part I and Part II of an application for life insurance

- List the sources that underwriters use to obtain additional medical, personal, and financial information about a proposed insured

- Describe the numerical rating system and explain how life underwriters use it to classify risks

- Identify the parties to a reinsurance agreement and state the general roles of each party

Outline of Major Topics

The Importance of Sound Underwriting
  Antiselection and Persistency
Organization of Underwriting
Underwriting Philosophy and Underwriting Guidelines
Fundamentals of Individual Life Insurance Underwriting
  Risk Assessment Factors
Fundamentals of Group Life Insurance Underwriting
  Risk Assessment Factors

Regulatory Requirements and Underwriting

Unfair Discrimination

Consumer Privacy

The Underwriting Process

Field Underwriting

Reviewing the Application for Insurance

Gathering Additional Information

Making an Underwriting Decision

Reinsuring Excess Risk

Basic Concepts of Reinsurance

Retention Limits

Case Studies

The case studies for this chapter are on the CD-ROM located on the inside back cover of this book.

Practice Questions

1. Jean Plymore works in the new business processing department of an insurance company. One of Ms. Plymore's responsibilities is to conduct suitability checks on insurance applications submitted to the insurer. The primary purpose of a suitability check is to ensure that the

    (1) application used is the correct form for the issuing jurisdiction
    (2) producer who submitted the application is properly licensed and appointed
    (3) insurance product applied for is appropriate for the applicant's needs
    (4) applicant has selected the most effective and efficient premium payment plan

2. In assessing the degree of risk represented by a proposed insured, an underwriter must be aware that people who suspect or know they are more likely than average to experience loss have a tendency to apply for or renew insurance protection to a greater extent than do people who lack such knowledge of probable loss. This underwriting concept is known as

    (1) suitability
    (2) mortality risk
    (3) antiselection
    (4) moral hazard

3. Judith Lawrence solicited an application from Leonard Petrov for an insurance policy covering the life of his wife Irina Petrov and submitted it, along with the policy's initial premium, to the Yardley Insurance Company. Kim Yee, a Yardley employee, reviewed the application, evaluated the risk, accepted the application, and determined the appropriate premium rate for the policy. The proposed insured in this transaction is

   (1) Judith Lawrence
   (2) Leonard Petrov
   (3) Irina Petrov
   (4) Kim Yee

4. Isaac Katz, an underwriter for the Valley Insurance Company, specializes in underwriting group life insurance plans. When making an underwriting decision on a group application, Mr. Katz consults Valley's *underwriting guidelines*, which are

   (1) general standards that specify the parameters within which proposed groups may be assigned to one of an insurer's risk classes established for each product
   (2) objectives that guide Valley's underwriting actions and reflect the company's strategic business goals and pricing assumptions
   (3) factors, such as age, sex, and medical history, that may affect a proposed group's level of mortality risk
   (4) decisions an underwriter makes regarding a group's risk classification and premium rate

5. An underwriter for the Cameo Insurance Company reviewed applications for life insurance coverage on the following proposed insureds:

   • Maria Alonzo, a 32-year-old female who has experienced a moderate weight gain over the last five years
   • Blain Morrisey, a 55-year-old male whose father died of a heart attack

   With regard to these two applications, it is correct to say that Cameo's underwriter most likely discovered risk factors that could increase the level of mortality risk represented by

   (1) both Ms. Alonzo and Mr. Morrisey
   (2) Ms. Alonzo only
   (3) Mr. Morrisey only
   (4) neither Ms. Alonzo nor Mr. Morrisey

6. Larry Oster, an underwriter for the Mayfair Insurance Company reviewed an application for insurance on the life of Rosalyn Belmont and assigned her to the substandard risk class. This information indicates that Mr. Oster considered Ms. Belmont's anticipated mortality to be

   (1) lower than average, and he charged her a lower-than-average premium rate
   (2) higher than average, and he charged her a higher-than-average premium rate
   (3) average, and he charged her an average premium rate
   (4) so great that Mayfair cannot provide coverage at an affordable rate

7. Most insurers in the United States would question the existence of insurable interest if a third-party application is submitted by a

    (1) close blood relative of the proposed insured
    (2) person closely related to the proposed insured by marriage
    (3) person financially indebted to the proposed insured
    (4) business partner of the proposed insured

8. The following statements are about risk assessment factors that underwriters consider when underwriting an application for group life insurance coverage. Select the answer choice containing the correct statement.

    (1) As a general rule, a small group tends to have fewer and smaller fluctuations in claims than does a large group.
    (2) A group that has a steady flow of new, younger members entering the group presents a lower risk than does a group whose membership remains unchanged over a long period of time.
    (3) Because women, as a group, exhibit lower mortality than do men, a group with a large proportion of women represents a statistically higher insurance risk than does a group with a large proportion of men.
    (4) Allowing part-time as well as full-time, permanent employees and their dependents to enroll in a group plan of life insurance reduces the possibility of antiselection.

9. In the United States, a group that is formed solely for the purpose of obtaining group insurance is known, for regulatory purposes, as a discretionary group. With respect to the issuance of insurance coverage to a discretionary group, it is correct to say that an insurer typically

    (1) can issue coverage to a discretionary group without restriction
    (2) can issue coverage to a discretionary group only if the insurer individually underwrites each member of the group
    (3) can issue coverage to a discretionary group only if the appropriate insurance regulatory authority specifically approves the policy for issuance to such a group
    (4) cannot issue coverage to a discretionary group under any circumstances

10. Group insurance plans can be either noncontributory plans or contributory plans. In a *noncontributory plan*, the insurer typically

    (1) establishes minimum participation requirements
    (2) provides automatic coverage to all eligible group members
    (3) requires group members to pay a portion of the premiums for their coverage
    (4) reduces the risk of antiselection by decreasing the likelihood that only people who have the greatest impairments will participate in the group policy

11. For this question, if answer choices (1) through (3) are all correct, select answer choice (4). Otherwise, select the one correct answer choice.

    Most jurisdictions in the United States have enacted laws that are designed to protect customers against unfair discrimination in underwriting. Generally, these unfair discrimination laws prohibit

    (1) an insurer from basing an underwriting decision on factors other than a proposed insured's health
    (2) an insurer from denying coverage to all proposed insureds who present a certain health impairment
    (3) an insurer from basing underwriting decisions on factors such as the proposed insured's sex, race, marital status, national origin, or religion
    (4) all of the above

12. Under certain circumstances, underwriters in the United States must follow procedures specified by the Fair Credit Reporting Act (FCRA). The FCRA regulates the reporting and use of information about a proposed insured's

    (1) personal finances that is provided by an insurance producer
    (2) personal medical history that is provided by an attending physician
    (3) hobbies and activities that is provided by the proposed insured's friends and neighbors
    (4) credit history that is provided by a consumer reporting agency

13. As an alternative to field underwriting, some insurers gather underwriting information through telephone interviews. This process, referred to as *teleunderwriting,* generally

    (1) eliminates the need for the applicant to complete an insurance application
    (2) allows third-party administrators (TPAs) rather than underwriters to approve insurance applications
    (3) increases the amount of information the producer must gather to make underwriting decisions
    (4) speeds the underwriting process

14. James Osgood met with an insurance producer to discuss the purchase of a life insurance policy on Mr. Osgood's life. During this meeting, Mr. Osgood completed a form that specified the amount and type of coverage he desired and provided basic information about his occupation, hobbies, aviation activities, driving record, criminal convictions, and existing life insurance coverage. Mr. Osgood and the producer then signed the form. The part of the insurance application that Mr. Osgood completed and signed is traditionally known as

    (1) Part I, which becomes part of the insurance contract
    (2) Part I, which is not part of the insurance contract
    (3) Part II, which becomes part of the insurance contract
    (4) Part II, which is not part of the insurance contract

15. An insurer's decision whether to require a medical report, nonmedical supplement, or paramedical report in an application for life insurance generally is based on the insurer's nonmedical limits. One characteristic of these nonmedical limits is that they

   (1) are the same for applicants in all age categories
   (2) apply only to the amount of insurance coverage requested on the application
   (3) describe the total amount of life insurance that the insurer will issue on a proposed insured without requiring a medical examination
   (4) determine the amount of nonmedical information about the proposed insured that the insurer requires

16. Underwriters in the United States and Canada often request information about proposed insureds from MIB Group, Inc. (MIB). One characteristic of MIB reports is that they

   (1) are generally used as the sole basis for making underwriting decisions
   (2) contain coded information about impairments that applicants have disclosed or that other insurance companies have detected in connection with previous applications for insurance
   (3) can be obtained and used without the proposed insured's written consent
   (4) become part of the insurance application

17. An insurance producer for the Pleasant Life Insurance Company received applications for life insurance from Jerome Dixon and Emily Pratt. The producer submitted both applications to Pleasant at a standard premium rate. After reviewing the applications, Pleasant's underwriter approved Mr. Dixon's coverage, but charged him a substandard premium rate. The underwriter approved coverage for Ms. Pratt at a standard rate, but reduced the amount of coverage the policy provided. With regard to these applications, it is correct to say that Pleasant's underwriter rated

   (1) both Mr. Dixon's application and Ms. Pratt's application
   (2) Mr. Dixon's application only
   (3) Ms. Pratt's application only
   (4) neither Mr. Dixon's application nor Ms. Pratt's application

18. The following statements are about the numerical rating system. Select the answer choice containing the correct statement.

   (1) The lower the numerical rating for a proposed insured, the higher the degree of mortality risk the proposed insured represents.
   (2) The numerical rating assigned to an individual proposed insured is used to determine the appropriate risk class for the individual.
   (3) Factors that have been determined statistically to increase a proposed insured's mortality risk receive negative values that are subtracted from a base value.
   (4) Only medical risk factors are used to calculate a numerical rating for a proposed insured's mortality risk.

19. For this question, if answer choices (1) through (3) are all correct, select answer choice (4). Otherwise, select the one correct answer choice.

    The actions necessary to complete an insurance transaction and put the purchased insurance coverage in force include

    (1) completion of an application for insurance
    (2) payment of the policy's initial premium
    (3) acceptance of the issued policy by the applicant
    (4) all of the above

20. The Bosworth Insurance Company and the Zenith Insurance Company entered into a reinsurance treaty. Under the terms of their agreement, Bosworth assumes up to $100,000 of risk on the policies it sells and Zenith assumes any risk on those policies in excess of $100,000. In the reinsurance relationship between Bosworth and Zenith, Bosworth is considered to be the

    (1) ceding company
    (2) retrocessionaire
    (3) reinsurer
    (4) assuming company

21. Under the terms of a reinsurance treaty, the reinsurer typically receives a premium from the ceding company as compensation for assuming the risk. For individual policies, the reinsurance premium is typically

    (1) the same for all risks transferred by the ceding company
    (2) payable on the entire amount of the issued policy
    (3) a flat amount based on the age and sex of the insured
    (4) expressed as a rate per $1,000 of risk reinsured

22. To help underwriters determine how much financial risk the insurer can assume on a person or group, insurers typically establish retention limits. An insurer's retention limit is the maximum amount of

    (1) coverage the insurer will issue to an individual applicant
    (2) insurance the insurer will carry at its own risk
    (3) risk the insurer can transfer to a reinsurer
    (4) benefit the insurer is legally responsible for paying to a policy beneficiary

Answers to Practice Questions begin on page 95.
Answer choice explanations are available on the CD-ROM on the inside back cover of this book.

CHAPTER 11

Customer Service

Chapter Objectives

After studying this chapter, you should be able to

- ■ Identify the various customers of an insurance company

- ■ Discuss which employees in an insurance company provide customer service

- ■ Define the term *customer contact center*

- ■ List the characteristics of effective customer service

- ■ List and describe some typical customer service transactions for individual life insurance and annuities

- ■ Describe how insurers evaluate the timeliness and quality of their customer service

- ■ Explain the meaning and purpose of *customer relationship management* (CRM)

- ■ Describe the types of information included in a comprehensive customer profile

Outline of Major Topics

Insurance Company Customers
    External Customers
    Internal Customers
    Insurance Producers

Who Provides Customer Service?

Why Is Customer Service So Important?

Effective Customer Service
    The Changing Role of Customer Service Representatives

Customer Service Transactions for Individual Life Insurance and Annuities
    Policyowner Information Changes
    Changes in Ownership of the Policy
    Annuitant and Annuity Date Changes
    Beneficiary Changes
    Premium Payment Changes

Case Studies

The case studies for this chapter are on the CD-ROM located on the inside back cover of this book.

Practice Questions

1. Laura Raleigh's responsibilities as a customer service representative (CSR) for an insurance company include providing service to the company's internal and external customers. Ms. Raleigh is providing service to an *internal* customer when she

    (1) contacts a policyowner whose producer retired and assigns the policyowner to a new producer
    (2) notifies one of the company's career agents that a client has decided to replace his existing policy with a policy from another company
    (3) sends a policy form for a new insurance product to the state insurance commissioner
    (4) calculates the amount of tax payable on a withdrawal requested by an annuity contract owner

2. To be effective, the service a company delivers to its customers must be prompt, complete, courteous, and accurate. By definition, customer service is *complete* if it

    (1) is delivered in a timely manner
    (2) improves the company's profitability
    (3) allows customer service employees to satisfy customers' service expectations
    (4) resolves a customer's problem or inquiry to the customer's satisfaction

3. Gordon Fuller, a CSR for an insurance company, received a transaction request from Sherry Stringer, one of the company's policyowners. When Mr. Fuller searched the company's policy records, he discovered that Ms. Stringer's policy had been assigned. This information indicates that Ms. Stringer had

   (1) changed her name on the policy as a result of a marriage or divorce
   (2) designated a new beneficiary on her policy
   (3) transferred some or all of her ownership rights in the policy to another party
   (4) instructed the insurer to begin using funds withdrawn from her bank account to pay her policy premiums

4. Elena Vargas, a CSR at an insurance company, received a request from a policyowner to decrease the amount of coverage provided by his life insurance policy. Ms. Vargas sent the policyowner the forms necessary to make the change. When she received the completed forms, Ms. Vargas added an amendment to the policy that limited the benefits payable under the policy. The method Ms. Vargas used to change the policyowner's coverage is known as

   (1) a policy rider
   (2) a fund reallocation
   (3) an automatic payment plan
   (4) a proactive transaction

5. Kaneesha Carter, an insurance company CSR, received notification that a policyowner wished to terminate his current annuity contract and use the money to purchase a life insurance policy from a different insurer. After verifying the request with the policyowner and the producer who sold the original policy, Ms. Carter terminated the original policy in the insurer's records, calculated the contract's net cash surrender value, and transferred funds in that amount to the policyowner. This information indicates that Ms. Carter processed the type of transaction known as

   (1) a policy reinstatement
   (2) an external replacement
   (3) a Section 1035 exchange
   (4) a private placement

6. To help ensure that it delivers timely customer service, the Bangor Insurance Company set a goal of connecting all inbound callers with a CSR in an average of one minute. This one-minute time limit is a benchmark Bangor uses to evaluate its

   (1) average speed of answer
   (2) rate of first-contact resolution
   (3) turnaround time
   (4) abandonment rate

7. As part of its customer relationship management (CRM) strategy, the Argosy Insurance Company creates comprehensive customer profiles for all of its customers. One type of information included in these customer profiles is a description of the customer's *wallet share*, which is

    (1) the economic benefit of the relationship between Argosy and its customers calculated over time

    (2) all of the products a customer has purchased from Argosy or one of its affiliates

    (3) the total of all past interactions between Argosy and the customer

    (4) the percentage of a customer's business on a particular type of product that the customer places with Argosy

Answers to Practice Questions begin on page 95.
Answer choice explanations are available on the CD-ROM on the inside back cover of this book.

CHAPTER

12 Claim and Annuity Benefit Administration

Chapter Objectives

After studying this chapter, you should be able to

- Explain the purpose of a life insurer's claim philosophy

- Describe the people involved in life insurance claim administration

- List and describe the basic activities in the life insurance claim decision process

- Explain how coverage exclusions in a life insurance policy can affect a claim decision

- Define *material misrepresentation* and explain how an insurer handles a material misrepresentation

- Discuss the actions that a claim analyst takes when approving and denying life insurance claims

- Describe the purpose and procedures for a claim investigation

- Explain the duties of the ceding company and the reinsurer when a claim is filed under an insurance policy that has been reinsured

- Describe how an insurance company administers annuity death benefits and scheduled periodic payments

Outline of Major Topics

The Life Insurance Claim Administration Function
    Claim Philosophy
    Claim Staff
    Regulation of Claim Administration

The Life Insurance Claim Decision Process
    Verification of Policy Status
    Verification of Coverage of the Insured
    Verification of the Loss
    Verification of Policy Coverage of the Loss
    Handling Contestable Claims
    Making a Claim Decision

Life Insurance Claim Investigation

    Claim Fraud

    Confidentiality

Claims on Reinsured Policies

    Notification of Claims

    Claim Decisions

Administration of Annuity Policy Benefits

    Annuity Death Benefit Administration

    Annuity Payout Administration

Case Studies

The case studies for this chapter are on the CD-ROM located on the inside back cover of this book.

Practice Questions

1. The following statements describe interactions between an insurance company's claim administration department and its customers. Select the answer choice describing an interaction that would be considered an unfair claim settlement practice under the National Association of Insurance Commissioners (NAIC) Model Unfair Claims Settlement Practices Act.

    (1) Marie Kensington, a claim analyst, hired an outside investigator to verify information related to a beneficiary's claim for life insurance policy proceeds.
    (2) Garth Giske, a claim analyst, authorized a settlement on a life insurance claim in an amount that was substantially less than the amount actually due under the policy.
    (3) After reviewing a claim for accidental death benefits, Maxine Harmon, a claim analyst, determined that the claimant had misinterpreted the policy's accidental death benefit provision and denied the claim.
    (4) Trent Jeffers, an analyst trainee, unknowingly failed to complete his first claim investigation within the required amount of time after receiving proof of loss.

2. Although verifying proof of loss is routine in most cases, a claim analyst would typically conduct further investigation in a situation in which the insured

    (1) was aboard a boat that sank during a storm, and no bodies were recovered
    (2) disappeared under unverifiable circumstances and the claimant submitted a court order stating that the insured is presumed dead in place of a death certificate
    (3) died outside of the country in which the policy was issued
    (4) died by suicide after the policy's suicide exclusion period expired

3. Antoine Blake purchased a whole life insurance policy from the Barnard Insurance Company on June 12, 2002. The policy contained a typical two-year suicide exclusion period. On August 23, 2004, Mr. Blake committed suicide. At the time of his death, no policy loans were outstanding. In this situation, the beneficiary of Mr. Blake's policy was entitled to receive

    (1) no payment of any kind
    (2) a refund of all premiums paid only
    (3) the policy's net cash surrender value only
    (4) the policy's full death benefit

4. On July 10, 2003, Michael York, a United States resident, purchased a variable life insurance policy on his life. The policy included a typical two-year contestable period. Mr. York died on August 20, 2004, and shortly thereafter, the policy beneficiary filed a claim for the policy's death benefit. At the time of Mr. York's death, the policy was still in force and there were no outstanding policy loans. While reviewing the claim, the insurer's claim examiner discovered that Mr. York had made a material misrepresentation on his application. In this situation, the insurer is liable for paying the policy beneficiary

    (1) nothing
    (2) the policy's net investment income
    (3) the premiums paid for the policy
    (4) the policy's face amount

5. Sherman Hinton, the beneficiary of a $100,000 life insurance policy, submitted a claim for policy proceeds. The claim analyst reviewing Mr. Hinton's claim noted that the policyowner had paid $250 in policy premiums in advance and that the policy had an unpaid policy loan of $5,000. Accrued interest on the loan was $100. This information indicates that the correct benefit amount payable to Mr. Hinton on his claim is

    (1) $94,900
    (2) $95,150
    (3) $100,000
    (4) $100,350

6. When Elizabeth Mason applied for an insurance policy on her life, she listed her age as 38. The policy included a typical two-year contestable clause and a two-year suicide exclusion provision. Ms. Mason died in an automobile accident 18 months after her policy went into effect. The claim analyst reviewing the claim for policy proceeds discovered that Ms. Mason had misstated her age on her insurance application and that she was really 45 years of age at the time she purchased her policy. In this situation, the claim analyst most likely will

   (1) deny the claim and make no payment to the policy beneficiary
   (2) return the premiums paid for the policy to the beneficiary
   (3) declare the policy void on the ground of a material misrepresentation in the insurance application
   (4) reduce the benefit to the amount that the premiums paid would have purchased at Ms. Mason's correct age

7. James Thurgood purchased an insurance policy on his life from the Clairmont Insurance Company and named his son, Adam, as policy beneficiary. When Mr. Thurgood died, Adam was still legally a minor, so the policy proceeds were left on deposit with the insurer. Clairmont's claim analyst sent Adam a notice that specified the minimum interest rate that Clairmont would pay on the proceeds and the frequency with which the interest payments would be made. The notice Clairmont's claim analyst sent to Adam is known as

   (1) a claimant's statement
   (2) a statement of indebtedness
   (3) an installment certificate
   (4) an authorization to release information

8. An insurance claim analyst who has reason to doubt some aspect of a life insurance claim may conduct a claim investigation. The primary purpose of this investigation is to

   (1) determine the amount payable on the claim
   (2) reduce the cost of administering the claim
   (3) obtain any additional information the analyst needs to reach a claim decision
   (4) transfer responsibility for determining the proper recipient of policy proceeds to a court

9. The following statements are about claims on reinsured policies. Select the answer choice containing the correct statement.

   (1) Like the ceding company, the reinsurer receives claims from and makes claim payments directly to the beneficiary of the underlying insurance contract.
   (2) When a claim on a reinsured policy is filed, the ceding company must receive payment from the reinsurer for the reinsured amount before it can pay the policy proceeds to the beneficiary.
   (3) Although the reinsurer can make claim decision recommendations to the ceding company, the ceding company is not required to follow these recommendations.
   (4) Most reinsurance treaties allow the ceding company to notify the beneficiary of a decision to approve or deny a claim without obtaining the reinsurer's approval of the decision.

10. The following statements are about annuity death benefit administration. Select the answer choice containing the correct statement.

    (1) Insurers typically do not require the beneficiary of an annuity contract to provide proof of loss to claim the contract's death benefit.
    (2) Most variable annuity contracts provide a death benefit equal to at least the amount of premiums paid, minus any withdrawals.
    (3) The beneficiary of an annuity contract is responsible for calculating the amount of the death benefit payment that is taxable and for reporting the taxable amount to the appropriate tax authorities.
    (4) Death benefits under annuity contracts are always payable as a lump sum to the contract beneficiary.

11. Distributions from annuity contracts can be classified as nonannuitized distributions or annuitized distributions. An example of an *annuitized* distribution is a

    (1) fixed-period distribution option
    (2) lump-sum distribution option
    (3) fixed-amount distribution option
    (4) joint and survivor payout option

Answers to Practice Questions begin on page 95.
Answer choice explanations are available on the CD-ROM on the inside back cover of this book.

CHAPTER 13 Information Management

Chapter Objectives

After studying this chapter, you should be able to

- Discuss the importance of effective information management for insurance companies and the characteristics of valuable information

- Describe the key elements of a computer-based information system

- List some types of application software commonly used by life insurers

- Discuss the security measures that insurers take to protect their information

- Explain the purpose of a transaction processing system and list some insurance activities often handled by transaction processing systems

- Describe how decision support systems and expert systems can help insurers solve problems and make business decisions

- Explain the functions of a database management system, a document management system, and an automated workflow system

- Discuss some of the ways insurers engage in electronic commerce

- Describe some of the computer and telecommunications technologies used to manage information for each of the following company functions: marketing, new business processing, underwriting, customer service, life insurance claim administration, and annuity benefit administration

Outline of Major Topics

Operations Support Technologies
 Database Management Systems
 Document Management Systems
 Automated Workflow Systems
Electronic Commerce
 Insurance Company Web Sites
 Business-to-Business e-Commerce
Information Management for Specific Company Functions
 Marketing
 New Business Processing
 Customer Service
 Life Insurance Claim Administration
 Annuity Benefit Administration

Case Studies

The case studies for this chapter are on the CD-ROM located on the inside back cover of this book.

Practice Questions

1. Computer-based information systems consist of hardware and software components. One of the critical elements in an information system is a central processing unit (CPU). A CPU is a form of computer

    (1) software that helps users perform specific tasks or solve particular types of problems
    (2) software that coordinates the activities and functions of the system
    (3) hardware that processes and manipulates data
    (4) hardware that ensures that instructions from users are sent accurately and efficiently to various system components

2. The Shoreline Insurance Company uses a type of software that performs calculations such as experience studies, profitability projections, cash values, and statutory reserve valuations. This software is an example of

    (1) illustration software, which is a type of application software
    (2) illustration software, which is a type of systems software
    (3) actuarial software, which is a type of application software
    (4) actuarial software, which is a type of systems software

3. The Overton Insurance Company facilitates communications between the home office and agency offices located throughout Overton's marketing territory through a network of computers linked by telecommunications hardware and software. The computer network that Overton operates is an example of

    (1) a local area network (LAN)
    (2) a wide area network (WAN)
    (3) a virtual private network (VPN)
    (4) an electronic data interchange (EDI) network

4. The Tetrad Insurance Company protects the information in its information system by means of an encryption system. The function of an encryption system is to

    (1) create an electronic barrier between the public and private areas of the company's information system
    (2) monitor system traffic and identify sequences of commands that indicate an unauthorized user is attempting to access the system
    (3) detect viruses and prevent them from infecting network computers
    (4) encode data so that only an authorized person possessing the required hardware and/or software can decode the data

5. The following statements describe types of information systems. Select the answer choice describing a transaction processing system.

    (1) The Able Insurance Company's information system includes an organized collection of hardware, software, databases, and procedures that managers use to make day-to-day decisions, control routine activities, and generate various financial reports.
    (2) The Eager Insurance Company's information system includes an organized collection of procedures, software, databases, and devices that allows Eager employees to handle activities such as application processing and policy issue and administration.
    (3) The Heavenly Insurance Company's information system includes hardware, software, databases, and procedures that help managers evaluate business situations, make decisions, and solve problems.
    (4) The Ingersoll Insurance Company's information system includes a group of computer programs that allow employees in various functional areas to access information in the company's customer information file (CIF) all at the same time using different computer programs.

6. Edward Markham, a sales manager for the Kensington Insurance Company, meets with his sales force each Friday. Mr. Markham has programmed the company's management information system (MIS) to provide him with reports summarizing weekly sales and commissions prior to each meeting. The reports Mr. Markham receives are known as

    (1) scheduled reports
    (2) exception reports
    (3) ad hoc reports
    (4) customer information files

7. Insurance company information systems incorporate different forms of computer technology that support operations. One of these technologies is data mining, which is the

   (1) process of converting printed characters or graphics into digital images
   (2) analysis of large amounts of data to discover previously unknown trends, patterns, and relationships
   (3) computer-to-computer exchange of data between organizations using a data format agreed upon by the sending and receiving parties
   (4) use of the Internet and other computer networks to deliver commercial information and to facilitate business transactions

8. The following statements are about electronic commerce (e-commerce). Select the answer choice containing the correct statement.

   (1) Most of the information included in insurance company Web sites is customized for individual site visitors.
   (2) The Internet is typically considered to be more secure than intranets and extranets because it includes firewalls and other security features that separate private and public information.
   (3) E-commerce is simply the sale of products and services over the Internet.
   (4) E-commerce eliminates some of the limitations of traditional commerce.

9. The Claymore Insurance Company allows applicants for life insurance to file applications electronically rather than on paper. If an application contains incomplete information or if benefit or premium amounts are outside acceptable limits, a software function prompts the applicant to provide additional information or to select a different benefit or premium amount. This software function is known as

   (1) a screen pop
   (2) an edit
   (3) a call me button
   (4) an exception report

10. Most insurers that use automated systems for claim administration program their systems to

   (1) make claim decisions on all claims, regardless of the type or amount of coverage
   (2) make claim decisions on claims that fall within certain predetermined limits, and refer claims that fall outside those limits to claim analysts
   (3) make claim decisions on claims that fall outside certain predetermined limits, and refer claims that fall inside those limits to claim analysts
   (4) refer all claim decisions to claim analysts

Answers to Practice Questions begin on page 95.
Answer choice explanations are available on the CD-ROM on the inside back cover of this book.

CHAPTER 14

An Overview of Financial Management

Chapter Objectives

After studying this chapter, you should be able to

■ List the general responsibilities of financial management in a life insurance company

■ Describe the types of information included in an insurer's balance sheet and income statement

■ Explain the importance of solvency and profitability

■ List the types of contingency risks that typically affect an insurer's solvency

■ List some of the ways that insurers measure solvency and profitability

■ Explain the basic steps involved in managing an insurance company's capital and surplus

■ Identify the basic cash inflows and cash outflows for an insurance company, and describe how cash flow affects solvency and profitability

■ Explain the basic objectives of asset/liability management (ALM)

■ Explain the importance of cash-flow testing

Outline of Major Topics

The Responsibilities and Organization of Financial Management
Basic Accounting Documents
  Balance Sheet
  Income Statement
  Linking the Income Statement to the Balance Sheet
Solvency and Profitability
  Solvency
  Profitability
Planning Financial Goals and Strategies
  Financial Goals
  Financial Strategies
  Measuring Financial Results
Managing the Insurer's Capital and Surplus
Managing Cash Flows
  The Effect of Cash Flows on Solvency and Profitability
  Asset/Liability Management

Case Studies

The case studies for this chapter are on the CD-ROM located on the inside back cover of this book.

Practice Questions

1. An accountant for the Sequoia Insurance Company is preparing the company's year-end financial statements. One of the values the accountant will include is an amount for the company's policy reserves. Policy reserves are classified as

    (1) expenses, and are included in Sequoia's balance sheet
    (2) expenses, and are included in Sequoia's income statement
    (3) liabilities, and are included in Sequoia's balance sheet
    (4) liabilities, and are included in Sequoia's income statement

2. An insurer can use the basic accounting equation to mathematically express the relationship among assets, liabilities, and capital and surplus. This equation states that a company's

    (1) Assets = Liabilities + Capital and surplus
    (2) Assets = Capital and surplus – Liabilities
    (3) Liabilities = Assets + Capital and surplus
    (4) Liabilities = Capital and surplus – Assets

3. The Sand Dollar Insurance Company recorded the following values on its income statement for the year ended December 31:

    - Premium income $1,000,000
    - Net investment income $250,000
    - Increase in policy reserves $50,000
    - Policy benefits and claims $750,000
    - Producer commissions $150,000
    - Operating expenses $100,000

    This information indicates that, for the year ended December 31, Sand Dollar had a

    (1) net income of $200,000
    (2) net income of $250,000
    (3) net loss of $200,000
    (4) net loss of $250,000

4. An insurance company's income statement is linked to its balance sheet at the end of each accounting period in that a net income at the end of the accounting period will result in

    (1) a decrease in both the company's capital and surplus and its assets
    (2) a decrease in the company's capital and surplus and an increase in its assets
    (3) an increase in the company's capital and surplus and a decrease in its assets
    (4) an increase in both the company's assets and its capital and surplus

5. Solvency is one of the major financial goals of most insurance companies. For an insurer, solvency refers to the

    (1) degree to which a company's revenues exceed its expenses during a defined period of time
    (2) overall degree of success a business has in generating returns for its owners
    (3) company's ability to maintain capital and surplus at or above the minimum standard required by law
    (4) reward or compensation that the company receives for taking risks

6. In the normal course of conducting its business, an insurer faces potentially serious risks that can threaten its solvency. These risks are known as contingency risks, or C risks. One type of C risk is the risk that an insurer's investments in stocks, bonds, mortgages, and real estate will lose value as a result of changes in market interest rates. This type of C risk is known as

    (1) asset risk (C-1 risk)
    (2) pricing risk (C-2 risk)
    (3) interest rate risk (C-3 risk)
    (4) general management risk (C-4 risk)

7. According to standards specified by the National Association of Insurance Commissioners (NAIC), a state insurance commissioner is required to place an insurer in receivership if the results of the insurer's risk-based capital (RBC) ratio calculations fall below 70 percent. When an insurer is placed in receivership, the state insurance commissioner of the state of domicile

    (1) requires the insurer to perform additional analyses
    (2) takes control of and administers the insurer's assets and liabilities
    (3) requires the insurer to submit a confidential plan of action
    (4) subjects the insurer to a confidential investigation

8. Insurers frequently use the return on capital ratio to measure profitability. The purpose of the return on capital ratio is to

    (1) compare some measure of an insurer's earnings during a stated period to some measure of its capital and surplus
    (2) allow the insurer to use information only from its income statement
    (3) determine the minimum percentage rate of return on capital that an insurer must earn for a given level of risk
    (4) express an insurer's profitability as an equation in which the insurer's return on capital is equal to the insurer's capital divided by its surplus

9. The following statements describe financial goals set by insurance companies. Select the answer choice describing a *solvency* goal.

   (1) The Bascomb Insurance Company established a goal of earning a 10 percent rate of return on capital for its line of life insurance products.
   (2) The Longmont Insurance Company set a goal of increasing the value of its assets by 5 percent over the next year.
   (3) The Oakley Insurance Company set a goal of maintaining or improving its industry rating.
   (4) The Paragon Insurance Company set a goal of increasing the share price of its stock by 3 percent.

10. The life insurance business involves both cash inflows and cash outflows. The pattern of an insurance company's cash flows

   (1) directly affects the company's solvency and profitability
   (2) directly affects the company's solvency, but has only an indirect effect on its profitability
   (3) directly affects the company's profitability, but has only an indirect effect on its solvency
   (4) has only an indirect effect on both the company's solvency and its profitability

11. One technique insurance companies use as part of asset/liability management (ALM) is forecasting. Managers can use forecasts to

   (1) calculate the company's current capital and surplus
   (2) predict the future behavior of various types of investments
   (3) identify the timing and amount of current cash flows into and out of the company
   (4) compare the company's existing asset and liability cash flows and its past cash flows

Answers to Practice Questions begin on page 95.
Answer choice explanations are available on the CD-ROM on the inside back cover of this book.

CHAPTER

15 Managing Investments

Chapter Objectives

After studying this chapter, you should be able to

■ Identify who is responsible for establishing an insurer's investment policy and describe the factors typically included in the investment policy

■ Explain the risk-return tradeoff in investing

■ Explain the meaning of *diversification* and why diversification of investments is important

■ Describe the regulation of insurer investments

■ Explain the difference between debt assets and equity assets, and give examples of each

■ List and describe the types of assets in which insurance companies typically invest

■ Describe the characteristics that determine the degree of risk associated with a bond

■ Describe the characteristics of conservative investment strategies and aggressive investment strategies

Outline of Major Topics

Organization of Investment Operations
    Establishing an Investment Policy
    Investment Department Activities
Returns on Insurer Investments
    Forms of Return
    Return and Risk
    Return, Inflation, and Deflation
    Return and Diversification
Regulation of Insurer Investments
Insurance Company Investments
    Buying and Selling Securities
    Bonds
    Stock
    Mortgages
    Real Estate
    Policy Loans
Investment Strategies

Case Studies

The case studies for this chapter are on the CD-ROM located on the inside back cover of this book.

Practice Questions

1. An investment policy typically incorporates an insurer's investment objectives, including maintaining an adequate spread. By definition, an insurer's spread is the

    (1) amount by which an asset's selling price exceeds its purchase price
    (2) difference between the rate of return earned on an insurer's investments and the interest rate credited on its products
    (3) excess of the insurer's revenues over its expenses during a defined period of time
    (4) excess of the insurer's investment income over its investment expenses

2. The following statements are about returns on insurers' investments. Select the answer choice containing the correct statement.

    (1) Through the investment strategy of diversification, the losses of one investment can be offset by the gains of other investments.
    (2) When an investment is earning a positive return, simultaneous high inflation generally causes the value of the investment to decrease along with the overall level of prices in the economy.
    (3) Because of the relationship between risk and return, an insurer that takes on considerable risk when making an investment can expect to be compensated with a lower return.
    (4) Simple interest earned on an insurer's investment is interest paid on both the original sum of money invested and on any previously accumulated interest.

3. A separate account (segregated fund) is an account that a life insurance company maintains apart from its general account. A life insurer establishes a separate account in order to

    (1) ensure that the life insurer will maintain the net amount of cash that an insurance product has accumulated per unit of coverage at any given time
    (2) maintain records of the assets that are pledged as security for a loan until the debt obligation is satisfied
    (3) support the liabilities associated with the variable products the life insurer has issued, such as variable life insurance policies and variable annuities
    (4) maintain the portion of the insurer's earnings that is available for distribution to owners of participating policies

4. One way for insurers and other large institutional investors to purchase new issues of securities is through a method in which the security is sold directly from the issuer to an institutional investor. Securities issued under this method are not required to be registered with government agencies, and an investment bank is not needed to facilitate the offering. This method of issuing new securities is known as

   (1) a public offering
   (2) a securities exchange
   (3) an over-the-counter (OTC) market
   (4) a private placement

5. The Nocturnal Insurance Company purchased a bond with a 9 percent coupon rate when the bond was issued. The bond will mature in 20 years, at which time the issuer will pay the bondholder $1,000. The following statements are about Nocturnal's bond. Select the answer choice containing the correct statement.

   (1) The face value of Nocturnal's bond equals $1,000.
   (2) A rise in the market interest rates one year after the bond was issued would make Nocturnal's bond more valuable in the marketplace.
   (3) If the market interest rates fall to 8 percent one year after the bond was issued, then the coupon rate on Nocturnal's bond most likely would fall to 8 percent.
   (4) Nocturnal's bond will provide an annual income of $900.

6. With respect to investments in bonds, it is correct to say that

   (1) bonds are typically the smallest investment holding in an insurer's general account because they are relatively risky investments that have unpredictable cash-flow properties
   (2) bonds that are backed only by the full faith and credit of the issuer are known as secured bonds
   (3) bonds issued by the federal government are the safest of all bonds, because the federal government can always raise taxes and even print money to pay off its debts
   (4) convertible bonds have a higher risk than do comparable nonconvertible bonds and, therefore, have higher coupon rates than do comparable nonconvertible bonds

7. Two insurer investments are stocks and bonds. When comparing stock investments to bond investments, it generally is correct to say that

   (1) stocks are considered to be a form of financing for the issuing corporations, whereas bonds are not considered to be a form of financing for the issuing corporations
   (2) the cash-flow characteristics of stocks are more regular than are the cash-flow characteristics of bonds
   (3) stock prices tend to fluctuate far less than do bond prices
   (4) stockholders have a lower priority claim than do bondholders on the issuing company's assets if the issuing company goes out of business

8. Many insurers use mortgages as an investment tool. One characteristic of mortgages as an investment tool is that mortgages typically are

    (1) rated by a mortgage rating agency, so the default risk presented to an insurer by a mortgage is relatively easy to evaluate

    (2) considered to be variable-income investments, because the insurer receives interest payments of different amounts at regular intervals

    (3) secured debt instruments that protect the insurer's investment in the event of a default

    (4) more liquid as an investment than are bonds

9. The Lakeside Company sold a building it owned to the Beachview Insurance Company and then immediately leased the building back from Beachview. Lakeside is responsible for the maintenance and operation of the building, and Beachview receives regular income in the form of lease payments from Lakeside. This method of investing in real estate is known as a

    (1) sale-and-leaseback transaction, and the lessor is Lakeside

    (2) sale-and-leaseback transaction, and the lessor is Beachview

    (3) buy-and-hold strategy, and the lessor is Lakeside

    (4) buy-and-hold strategy, and the lessor is Beachview

10. The following statements are about life insurance policy loans. Select the answer choice containing the correct statement.

    (1) An outstanding policy loan and any accrued interest are deducted from the benefit payable when the insured person dies.

    (2) Policy loans require the borrower to establish a systematic repayment plan.

    (3) Policy loans generally have contractual maturity dates.

    (4) An insurer charges customers a rate of interest on policy loans that is higher than the rate of interest the insurer earns on other investments.

Answers to Practice Questions begin on page 95.
Answer choice explanations are available on the CD-ROM on the inside back cover of this book.

CHAPTER 16 Accounting

Chapter Objectives

After studying this chapter, you should be able to

- Give examples of the internal and external users of accounting information

- Describe the differences between financial accounting and management accounting

- Describe the differences between generally accepted accounting principles (GAAP) and statutory accounting practices in the United States, and explain how each set of accounting standards is used

- Name and describe the basic types of financial accounting operations in life insurance companies

- State the purposes of a U.S. Annual Statement and an annual report

- Explain how and why insurers prepare budgets and perform cost accounting

- Explain the purposes of auditing

Outline of Major Topics

Users of Accounting Information
    Internal Users
    External Users
Organization and Responsibilities of the Accounting Department
Financial Accounting
    Accounting Standards
    Financial Accounting Operations
    Financial Reporting
Management Accounting
    Budgeting
    Cost Accounting
Auditing

Case Studies

The case studies for this chapter are on the CD-ROM located on the inside back cover of this book.

Practice Questions

1. The users of an insurer's accounting information generally fall into two groups: internal users and external users. One example of an *external* user of an insurer's accounting information is

    (1) a member of the insurer's board of directors
    (2) the insurer's manager of product development
    (3) a career agent of the insurer
    (4) a policyowner of the insurer

2. A typical activity performed by a life insurer's accounting department is

    (1) evaluating the characteristics of a proposed investment
    (2) developing premium rates for insurance products
    (3) determining mortality rates for groups of insureds
    (4) assisting managers with the interpretation of financial results

3. The following statements are about financial accounting conducted in accordance with generally accepted accounting principles (GAAP) and statutory accounting practices in the United States. Select the answer choice containing the correct statement.

    (1) The Securities and Exchange Commission (SEC) requires all publicly traded companies and companies that sell variable life insurance or variable annuity products to prepare general-use financial statements according to statutory accounting practices.
    (2) GAAP focuses on demonstrating to regulators that an insurer is able to meet its policy obligations even under adverse circumstances, whereas statutory accounting practices are oriented more toward demonstrating an insurer's profitability.
    (3) Financial statements prepared according to GAAP provide users with financial information that is based on standardized definitions, valuation methods, and formats, which allows users to effectively evaluate the financial performance of one company from year to year and to compare the financial performances of several companies.
    (4) The underlying premise of financial statements prepared in accordance with statutory accounting practices is the going-concern concept, which bases accounting processes on the assumption that a company will continue to operate for an indefinite period of time.

4. The following statements are about financial accounting operations. Select the answer choice containing the correct statement.

   (1) When an investment matures or is sold, any gain on the investment is considered to be an unrealized gain.

   (2) Premium accounting systems are used to ensure that policyowners are properly billed and that premium payments from policyowners are properly accounted for, but such systems are not typically used to prepare financial statements and management accounting reports.

   (3) General accounting is the accounting operation that is responsible for recording all financial transactions related to the policies an insurer has issued, including accounting for policy loans and claim payments.

   (4) For financial reporting purposes related to premium taxes, insurers maintain separate accounting records of premiums for each country, state, and province in which they write business.

5. One financial statement that is used in financial reporting provides information about the company's cash receipts, cash disbursements, and net change in cash during a specified period. This type of financial statement is known as

   (1) a balance sheet
   (2) an income statement
   (3) a cash flow statement
   (4) a statement of owners' equity

6. For the purposes of Annual Statement reporting in the United States, life insurers divide their assets into three categories: admitted assets, partially admitted assets, and nonadmitted assets. From the answer choices below, select the response that correctly identifies the asset classification of investment-grade securities and accounts receivable due in 90 days or more.

	Investment-grade securities	Accounts receivable due in 90 days or more
(1)	admitted asset	partially admitted asset
(2)	admitted asset	nonadmitted asset
(3)	partially admitted asset	partially admitted asset
(4)	partially admitted asset	nonadmitted asset

7. In Canada, one financial document presents information about an insurer's operations and performance, with an emphasis on demonstrating the insurer's solvency. Life insurers that are subject to federal regulation are required to file this document with the Office of the Superintendent of Financial Institutions (OSFI) and with the provincial insurance regulators of each province in which they write business. This document is known as an

   (1) Annual Return, and it is prepared according to Canadian statutory accounting practices
   (2) Annual Return, and it is prepared according to Canadian GAAP
   (3) Annual Statement, and it is prepared according to Canadian statutory accounting practices
   (4) Annual Statement, and it is prepared according to Canadian GAAP

8. One difference between financial accounting and management accounting is that *management accounting*

    (1) is not subject to specific accounting principles, whereas financial accounting is subject to specific accounting principles
    (2) provides data for external users, whereas financial accounting provides data for internal users
    (3) reports only on the business as a whole, whereas financial accounting can focus on the business as a whole or on individual parts of the business
    (4) is required by law, whereas financial accounting is not required by law

9. One type of budget that an insurer typically prepares shows the insurer's plans for the financial management of long-term, high-cost investments, such as the purchase of another company or the launch of a new product. This type of budget is known as

    (1) a cash budget
    (2) a revenue budget
    (3) an operational budget
    (4) a capital budget

10. One method financial managers can use to analyze an insurer's costs is comparative analysis. By definition, comparative analysis is the process by which an insurer

    (1) links its costs to its products based on the activities required to produce each product
    (2) compares an expense in one period to the same expense in a different period to identify cost trends, fluctuations, peaks, and valleys
    (3) examines and evaluates company records and procedures to ensure that the company's financial statements are presented fairly and reasonably
    (4) accumulates costs to each company function and analyzes the costs of specific processes, such as policy issue and claim processing

11. The following statements are about auditing and financial condition examinations. Select the answer choice containing the correct statement.

    (1) If an insurer refuses to undergo a financial condition examination or to comply with reasonable requests from examiners, the insurer's license to conduct business in the jurisdiction may be suspended or not renewed.
    (2) In the United States, external audits are always voluntary activities for publicly traded insurers.
    (3) In the United States, insurers must undergo a financial condition examination at least every ten years.
    (4) The scope of an insurer's financial audit is limited to only one aspect of the insurer's finances, such as an examination of premium accounting.

Answers to Practice Questions begin on page 95.
Answer choice explanations are available on the CD-ROM on the inside back cover of this book.

CHAPTER 17 Human Resource Management

Chapter Objectives

After studying this chapter, you should be able to

■ Describe the functions of the human resources department

■ Describe how companies conduct human resource planning

■ Describe the steps involved in the employee selection process

■ Identify several different types of pre-employment tests

■ Discuss some types of employee training programs used by insurers

■ Describe several types of performance evaluation methods and the benefits and limitations of each one

■ Identify the factors considered when determining employee pay scales

■ Explain the role of the human resources area in employee separation

Outline of Major Topics

Human Resource Planning
    Projecting Staffing Needs
    Estimating the Labor Supply
    Planning for International Operations
Recruitment
    Internal Recruitment
    External Recruitment
Employee Selection
    Application and Screening
    Pre-Employment Testing
    Employment Interviews
    Background Checks and Drug Tests
Training
Performance Evaluation
    Graphic Rating Scale Appraisal

Essay Appraisal
       Critical Incident Evaluation
       Ranking
       Management by Objectives
       360-Degree Feedback
Compensation
       Pay Scales
       Benefits and Services
Employee Retention
Separation of Employees

Case Studies

The case studies for this chapter are on the CD-ROM located on the inside back cover of this book.

Practice Questions

1. In large life insurance companies, the human resources department often maintains a skills inventory on the company's staff. A skills inventory can be defined correctly as a

    (1) forecast of the impact of information technology development on the nature and size of the company's workforce
    (2) projection of the number of people inside and outside the company who might be able to fill certain types of positions
    (3) manual or computerized database that contains information about the education, training, and experience of each person working for the company
    (4) report examining employee turnover arising from resignations, retirements, and other voluntary and involuntary terminations

2. Host country staffing is one approach that insurers use to staff an international operation. One characteristic of host country staffing is that this approach to staffing usually

    (1) reduces the possibility of communication problems between the home office and the foreign office
    (2) can help improve relations with the host country by increasing employment opportunities for its citizens
    (3) ensures that the elements of the corporate culture of the home office will be maintained in the foreign office
    (4) increases the insurer's risk of losing employees who have a difficult time adjusting to living in the host country

3. Companies may use internal or external recruitment in order to fill job openings. Compared to internal recruitment, *external* recruitment typically will result in

   (1) a decrease in the cost of identifying and hiring new employees
   (2) an increase in the level of employee morale
   (3) an increase in current employees' experience and value, and often, their enthusiasm and loyalty
   (4) an increase in the potential for the organization to develop new ideas

4. Cynthia Waddell, an applicant for a clerical position at an insurance company, took an employment test that measures job-related skills, such as data entry, filing, and communication skills. She scored 90% on the test. In order to verify her performance, Ms. Waddell took another version of the same test three days later. Her score on the second test was 78%. The content and results of the test Ms. Waddell took indicate that the test is

   (1) both valid and reliable
   (2) valid, but not reliable
   (3) reliable, but not valid
   (4) neither valid nor reliable

5. Employers use a variety of pre-employment tests in order to select the best candidate for a job. The type of pre-employment test that attempts to evaluate how well a job applicant has mastered specific skills needed to perform well in the position is known as

   (1) a performance test
   (2) an aptitude test
   (3) a behavioral tendencies test
   (4) a cognitive abilities test

6. Companies have instituted a process of introducing a new employee to an organization's procedures, policies, culture, and other employees. This process, which is part of a company's employee training programs, is known as

   (1) benchmarking
   (2) accountability
   (3) positioning
   (4) orientation

7. The following statements are about the benefits and limitations of various employee training methods. Select the answer choice containing the correct statement.

   (1) One limitation of on-the-job training is that trainees who make errors may create problems the trainer must correct.
   (2) One limitation of classroom training is that its informal structure can lead to inconsistencies in training.
   (3) The primary benefit of self-study training is that it provides each trainee with real work training and personalized attention.
   (4) One benefit associated with classroom training is that it helps the trainee build relationships with coworkers.

8. The following statements describe situations in which a life insurance company uses a particular performance evaluation method to evaluate its employees. Select the answer choice that correctly describes the use of the graphic rating scale appraisal method.

    (1) Supervisors at the Kingston Life Insurance Company record examples of each employee's accomplishments, as well as any errors or problems that occurred during the evaluation period, and uses these examples to evaluate the employee's performance.
    (2) At the Windmill Life Insurance Company, supervisors rate each employee's work during the evaluation period based on a number of job-related factors—such as "completes work on time," "maintains high standards," and "finds better ways to do work" —that were identified at the beginning of the appraisal period.
    (3) The manager of each department at the Maple Life Insurance Company compares department employees with one another and places them in order, from best to worst, based on specific characteristics of their work behavior or on overall performance.
    (4) Supervisors at the Cucumber Life Insurance Company evaluate each of their employees' strengths, weaknesses, accomplishments, and potential for promotion in a written description of the employee's job performance during a specified evaluation period.

9. At the beginning of each evaluation period, Gavin Spencer works with his supervisor to set clear and attainable goals that Mr. Spencer should achieve during the upcoming performance evaluation period and to develop a plan for achieving those goals. During the evaluation period, Mr. Spencer and his supervisor discuss Mr. Spencer's progress toward his goals. At the end of the period, they evaluate Mr. Spencer's success in meeting the goals, discuss any problems that occurred, and set goals for the next period. The performance evaluation method used by Mr. Spencer and his supervisor is known as

    (1) 360-degree feedback
    (2) critical incident evaluation
    (3) management by objectives (MBO)
    (4) a behaviorally anchored rating scale (BARS)

10. The primary reason that a company would provide outplacement counseling services to its employees would be to

    (1) attempt to discover an employee's typical job behaviors, such as whether the person is a team player, is honest, follows rules and procedures, and remains calm under pressure
    (2) provide career counseling, vocational testing and skills evaluation, and information about job searches to laid-off employees
    (3) provide an opportunity for a terminated employee to discuss the his or her opinions about working conditions at the company and ways of improving any problem areas
    (4) provide advice or counsel to help employees resolve ethical dilemmas and report ethical misconduct

Answers to Practice Questions begin on page 95.
Answer choice explanations are available on the CD-ROM on the inside back cover of this book.

Legal and Compliance Operations

Chapter Objectives

After studying this chapter, you should be able to

- ■ Discuss the legal department's role in various insurance company operations, such as incorporation and changes to corporate structure, product development, contracts, product distribution, and claim administration

- ■ Identify some of the important laws that govern employer-employee relationships for life insurance companies in the United States

- ■ Describe three important elements of a comprehensive compliance program

- ■ Describe some of the components of market conduct compliance for insurance companies in the United States

- ■ Explain the activities involved in an on-site market conduct examination

Outline of Major Topics

Case Studies

The case studies for this chapter are on the CD-ROM located on the inside back cover of this book.

Practice Questions

1. An insurance company's legal department must be skilled in several branches of the law. One body of law that affects an insurer's business governs the relationship between the insurer and producers who have been appointed to act on behalf of the insurer to sell the insurer's products. This type of law is known as

    (1) civil rights law
    (2) agency law
    (3) real property law
    (4) employment law

2. As employers, life insurance companies must abide by numerous laws that govern the relationship between an employer and an employee. In the United States, one such law is the Fair Labor Standards Act (FLSA). One purpose of the FLSA is to

    (1) establish minimum wage, overtime pay, record keeping, and child labor standards
    (2) ensure that certain minimum plan requirements are contained in employee welfare benefit plans established by employers
    (3) require employers to permit eligible employees in specific circumstances to take up to 12 weeks of unpaid leave within any 12-month period
    (4) prohibit employment discrimination on the basis of factors such as a person's race, national origin, color, religion, or sex

3. In the United States, federal laws prohibit employment discrimination. One such law protects people who are 40 years of age or older from being discriminated against in the workplace because of their age. This legislation is known as the

    (1) Fair Labor Standards Act (FLSA)
    (2) Americans with Disabilities Act (ADA)
    (3) Civil Rights Act of 1964
    (4) Age Discrimination in Employment Act (ADEA)

4. Typically, insurers try to settle legal disputes before cases go to trial. An insurer's legal department may offer to settle a dispute through a method of conflict resolution in which an impartial third party evaluates the facts in dispute and renders a decision that is binding on both parties. This dispute resolution process is known, by definition, as

    (1) litigation
    (2) compliance
    (3) arbitration
    (4) mediation

5. For this question, if answer choices (1) through (3) are all correct, select answer choice (4). Otherwise, select the one correct answer choice.

    To effectively meet their regulatory obligations, insurers typically establish internal control systems to encourage adherence to the company's compliance management policies, to promote operational efficiency, and to safeguard the organization's assets. Examples of an insurer's internal controls include

    (1) recalculating premiums charged to randomly selected policyowners
    (2) periodically sending to producers statements requesting notification of errors in payment
    (3) voiding, rather than discarding, checks that contain errors
    (4) all of the above

6. The following statements are about market conduct compliance in the United States. Select the answer choice containing the correct statement.

    (1) A market conduct examination is designed to identify and monitor threats to an insurer's solvency.
    (2) The National Association of Securities Dealers (NASD) administers federal securities laws, which govern all types of securities.
    (3) Insurance companies typically are not responsible for the conduct of their producers, regardless of the producer's relationship to the insurer.
    (4) A life insurer generally may not begin to sell an insurance product in a state until the product's policy form has been filed with and approved by the state insurance department.

7. The paragraph below contains two pairs of terms enclosed in parentheses. Determine which term in each pair correctly completes the paragraph. Then select the answer choice containing the two terms that you have chosen.

    The insurance department of State A notified the Palmtree Insurance Company that it wished to conduct a full-scope market conduct examination of Palmtree. The market conduct examination is the type known as a **(comprehensive / target)** examination and it will determine whether Palmtree's **(financial / nonfinancial)** operations are in compliance with applicable laws and regulations.

    (1) comprehensive / financial
    (2) comprehensive / nonfinancial
    (3) target / financial
    (4) target / nonfinancial

Answers to Practice Questions begin on page 95.
Answer choice explanations are available on the CD-ROM on the inside back cover of this book.

Answers to
Practice Questions

Answers to Practice Questions

Chapter 13

Chapter 14

Chapter 15

Chapter 16

Chapter 17

Chapter 18

Sample
Examination

This examination contains 75 objective questions. Each question is valued at 1.3333 points. For each question, circle the number of your chosen response.

1. The Muirfield Financial Services Company measures its customer service performance against established benchmarks. One component of customer service that Muirfield measures is the successful completion of a transaction, information, or service request at the initial point of contact with the customer. By definition, this component of customer service is known as

    (1) first-contact resolution
    (2) average handling time
    (3) average speed of answer
    (4) turnaround time

2. In addition to complying with certain federal laws, life insurance companies in the United States must comply with the laws of each state in which they do business. Specific regulatory issues that are typically overseen by a state insurance department rather than by the federal government include

    (1) the sale of securities
    (2) interstate advertising
    (3) the underwriting and claims practices of insurers
    (4) the establishment of anti-money laundering programs

3. The life insurance business involves many cash inflows and cash outflows. A cash *inflow* for an insurer would result from

    (1) a payment for an operating expense
    (2) the purchase of a new asset
    (3) the cash surrender of a life insurance policy by a policyowner
    (4) external financing

4. By definition, an organization that channels funds from those people, businesses, and governments that have a surplus of funds (savers) to those that have a shortage of funds (borrowers) is known as a

    (1) third-party administrator
    (2) lessor
    (3) principal
    (4) financial intermediary

5. In Canada, the federal government agency that regulates the solvency of federally incorporated companies, foreign insurers, and specified provincially incorporated insurers is the

    (1) Office of the Superintendent of Financial Institutions (OSFI)
    (2) Canadian Council of Insurance Regulators (CCIR)
    (3) Insurance Marketplace Standards Association (IMSA)
    (4) Canadian Life and Health Insurance Association (CLHIA)

6. The two most common types of commercial insurance companies are stock companies and mutual companies. With regard to these two types of insurance companies, it is generally correct to say that

   (1) stock companies guarantee preferred stockholders that they will receive stockholder dividends
   (2) the number of mutual insurers and the market share held by mutual insurers have increased in most countries over the past few decades
   (3) mutual insurers can purchase stock in a stock insurer but, because mutual insurers do not issue stock, they cannot be acquired by another company through the purchase of stock
   (4) mutual insurers are not permitted to issue nonparticipating life insurance policies

7. The organizational structure at the Stellar Insurance Company consists of three basic layers, with the middle layer being much narrower than the top and bottom layers. The top layer contains executives who are responsible for formulating Stellar's strategic plan. The middle layer consists of a small group of middle-level managers who coordinate the functions of the bottom layer, which consists of a diverse group of technical/professional employees. Stellar's middle-level managers are generalists rather than functional specialists. With respect to organizational shapes, this information indicates that Stellar is structured as

   (1) an hourglass organization
   (2) a network organization
   (3) a cluster organization
   (4) a traditional pyramid organization

8. The following statements describe insurance producers who are engaging in generally prohibited sales practices. Select the answer choice that best describes a producer who is engaging in the unfair sales practice known as *rebating*.

   (1) Monique Adair offered a prospect an inducement in the form of a cash payment to purchase a life insurance policy from her.
   (2) Lorenzo Garcia misrepresented the features of an insurance policy to induce a customer to replace her current insurance policy.
   (3) Nicholas Chan induced a customer to replace one annuity policy after another so that he could earn a series of commissions on the initial premiums for the replacements.
   (4) During a sales presentation, Shelly Fagan used a policy illustration that had not been approved for use by the insurer's home office and that gave the customer inaccurate information about a policy's premiums and cash values.

9. Kyle Vorsten, a career agent, holds an agency contract with the Zinnia Insurance Company, which is his primary insurance company. In addition to placing business with Zinnia, Mr. Vorsten can place business with other insurers with which he holds agency contracts. When Mr. Vorsten places business with an insurer *other than Zinnia*, Mr. Vorsten is functioning as

   (1) a general agent
   (2) a subagent
   (3) an agent-broker
   (4) an insurance aggregator

10. Bankinsurance involves the distribution of insurance products to a bank's own customers through the bank's distribution channels. Two strategies that banks typically use to market insurance products are third-party marketers (TPMs) and platform employees. With regard to these two types of marketing strategies, it is correct to say

    (1) that, in a TPM arrangement, the insurer's relationship is with the bank that provides the TPM with office space and access to the bank's customers, rather than with the TPM
    (2) that TPMs may be under contract to only one insurer at a time
    (3) that, in a platform employee arrangement, an insurer hires its own employees to sell the insurer's products from a bank
    (4) that, in a platform employee arrangement, the insurer compensates the bank, and then the bank compensates the platform employees for their insurance sales

11. One concept important to sound life insurance underwriting is the concept of antiselection. By definition, antiselection is the

    (1) possibility that an applicant or a proposed insured may intentionally be inaccurate about the proposed insured's current health, health history, activities and habits, or financial position
    (2) likelihood that, over a specified period, a percentage of an insurer's business will be terminated by policyowners
    (3) tendency of people to withdraw money from one financial intermediary and place the money with another financial intermediary to earn a higher return
    (4) tendency of people who suspect or know they are more likely than average to experience loss to apply for or renew insurance protection to a greater extent than are people who lack such knowledge of probable loss

12. There are several categories of risk, known as contingency risks or C risks, that may affect insurers' solvency. The risk category known as *asset risk (C-1 risk)* refers to the risk

    (1) of loss resulting from ineffective general business practices, such as inefficient management
    (2) that the insurer's experience with mortality or expenses will differ significantly from expectations, causing the insurer to lose money on its products, such as the risk that product-related expenses will increase
    (3) that market interest rates might shift, causing the insurer's assets to lose value and/or its liabilities to gain value, such as the risk that the insurer will incur a loss on the sale of a bond when interest rates rise
    (4) that the insurer will lose value on its investments for a reason *other than* a change in market interest rates, such as the risk that the issuer of bonds owned by an insurer will default and not make scheduled bond payments

13. As a new business processor at a life insurance company, Prabha Rai is responsible for conducting good order checks of life insurance applications and performing suitability checks to ensure that applications comply with state suitability requirements. Consider the following activities that Ms. Rai performed after receiving a life insurance application from a producer:

   - **Activity A**: She ensured that the application used is the correct form for the issuing state.
   - **Activity B**: She verified that the producer who submitted the application is properly licensed and appointed.
   - **Activity C**: She determined whether the applied-for insurance product is an appropriate purchase for the applicant, based on the applicant's financial needs.
   - **Activity D**: She established a policy record and arranged for special services as requested by the applicant.

   Ms. Rai performed the activity known as a *suitability check* when she performed

   (1) Activity A
   (2) Activity B
   (3) Activity C
   (4) Activity D

14. Vandelle Walker is the annuitant of an annuity which guarantees that annuity payments will be made throughout Ms. Walker's lifetime and that payments will continue for at least a specified period, even if she dies before the end of that period. Ms. Walker designated her son, Alfonzo, as the annuity's contingent payee. If Ms. Walker dies before the specified period expires, Alfonzo will receive annuity payments throughout the remainder of the specified period. This information indicates that Ms. Walker purchased the type of annuity known as a

   (1) joint and survivor annuity
   (2) life only annuity
   (3) life income with period certain annuity
   (4) life income with refund annuity

15. Three staffing options available to a multinational insurer are host country staffing, home country staffing, or staffing a foreign office with third-country nationals. One true statement about these staffing options for international operations is that

   (1) *host country staffing* involves placing staff members from the insurer's home country into the host country's workplace
   (2) *home country staffing* is less expensive for the multinational insurer than is host country staffing
   (3) *host country staffing* offers the advantage of using employees who are already familiar with the local customs, manners, and ways of doing business
   (4) staffing an office with *third-country nationals* eliminates the expense of relocating employees to the host country

16. In the United States, all publicly traded companies, including stock insurance companies, are subject to the federal Sarbanes-Oxley Act of 2002. One important requirement of the Sarbanes-Oxley Act is the

    (1) implementation of certain measures designed to detect and prevent illegal activities used to finance terrorism
    (2) inclusion of certain minimum plan requirements in employee welfare benefit plans
    (3) implementation of certain measures designed to maintain the privacy and security of consumers' personal health information
    (4) mandatory certification of the accuracy of a company's financial statements by the company's chief executive officer and chief financial officer

17. When the proceeds of a life insurance policy are left on deposit with an insurer, a claim analyst sends the beneficiary a document which specifies a minimum interest rate that the insurer will pay on the proceeds and the frequency with which the insurer will make interest payments to the beneficiary. This document is known as

    (1) a statement of indebtedness
    (2) a directive
    (3) a policy endorsement
    (4) an installment certificate

18. The following statements are about insurance producer compensation. Select the answer choice that contains the correct statement.

    (1) Under a level commission schedule, first-year commissions are higher than renewal commissions.
    (2) Insurance companies that use agency-building distribution systems to sell life insurance typically use the amount of first-year commissions earned as the production measure to determine whether producers qualify for security benefits.
    (3) A heaped commission schedule for life insurance products typically features relatively low first-year commissions and higher renewal commissions.
    (4) Under an asset-based commission schedule for annuities, the percentages of premium payments made by annuity policyowners are applied only to new premium payments rather than to the accumulated value and growth of an annuity policy's funds.

19. The users of an insurer's accounting information generally fall into one of two groups: internal users and external users. One example of an *external* user of an insurer's accounting information is a

    (1) company officer of the insurer
    (2) manager of the insurer's actuarial department
    (3) creditor of the insurer
    (4) member of the insurer's board of directors

20. As employers, life insurance companies in the United States must comply with federal laws that prohibit employment discrimination. One such law requires employers with 50 or more employees to allow eligible employees in specific circumstances to take up to 12 weeks of unpaid leave within any 12-month period. This employment law is known as the

    (1) Fair Labor Standards Act (FLSA)
    (2) Pregnancy Discrimination Act
    (3) Family and Medical Leave Act (FMLA)
    (4) Americans with Disabilities Act (ADA)

21. The following statements are about generally accepted accounting principles (GAAP) and statutory accounting practices. Select the answer choice that contains the correct statement.

    (1) Insurance companies in the United States must prepare their annual reports according to statutory accounting practices.
    (2) Statutory accounting practices are designed to provide insurance regulators with information about an insurer's solvency, whereas GAAP are oriented toward demonstrating an insurer's profitability.
    (3) Insurance companies that conduct business in more than one state must satisfy the statutory accounting requirements of only the state in which they are domiciled.
    (4) Generally, statutory accounting is perceived as a less conservative accounting approach than that of the going-concern concept used by GAAP.

22. Most information systems today are computer-based systems that consist, in part, of different types of software. One type of software is application software. With regard to application software, it is correct to say that it

    (1) is the equipment and mechanical devices included in a computer-based information system
    (2) consists of computer programs that help users perform specific tasks or solve particular types of problems
    (3) coordinates the activities and functions of the information system's hardware components
    (4) contains the computer circuitry that performs the processing or data manipulation activities

23. The Parkside Life Insurance Company prepared a budget that indicates the amount of income from policy sales and investments that Parkside expects in the coming budget period. Parkside prepared this budget first because the budget determines the financial limits of other budgets. In this situation, Parkside prepared the type of budget known as

    (1) a capital budget
    (2) an expense budget
    (3) a cash budget
    (4) a revenue budget

24. The Idyllic Life Insurance Company issued a $500,000 individual insurance policy covering the life of Raymond Travanti. Idyllic then transferred $200,000 of the risk on the $500,000 policy to the Mirage Insurance Company under the terms of a reinsurance treaty between the two insurers. The following statements are about this reinsurance arrangement. Select the answer choice that contains the correct statement.

    (1) Mr. Travanti has a contractual relationship with both Idyllic and Mirage.
    (2) In this reinsurance transaction, Idyllic is the ceding company, and Mirage is the retrocessionaire.
    (3) The $200,000 of insurance coverage that Idyllic transferred to Mirage represents Idyllic's retention limit.
    (4) The amount of the reinsurance premium for this policy most likely is based on Mr. Travanti's age and sex, whether he uses tobacco, and whether his risk classification is standard or substandard.

25. The following paragraph contains two pairs of terms enclosed in parentheses. Determine which term in each pair correctly completes the paragraph. Then select the answer choice containing the two terms that you have chosen.

    The organizational structure of a company can be described as having characteristics of centralization or decentralization. Centralized and decentralized organizations each have advantages. In general, it is correct to say that **(centralized / decentralized)** organizations provide lower-level managers with more authority to make decisions, thus allowing them to respond quickly to situations. **(Centralized / Decentralized)** organizations are more likely to have company policies that are consistent from one area of the company to the next.

    (1) centralized / Centralized
    (2) centralized / Decentralized
    (3) decentralized / Centralized
    (4) decentralized / Decentralized

26. Ming Phan is a producer for the Hightower Life Insurance Company. She accepted a life insurance application from Vanessa Crenshaw, who claimed on the application that she did not use tobacco products. Ms. Phan reported in a section of the application that she suspected Ms. Crenshaw did, in fact, smoke cigarettes. She based her suspicion on the fact that Ms. Crenshaw lives alone and that she saw full ashtrays and cigarette lighters in Ms. Crenshaw's house. The portion of the application that Ms. Phan most likely used to report her suspicion about Ms. Crenshaw's being a smoker is known as

    (1) a nonmedical supplement
    (2) the agent's statement
    (3) Part I of the application
    (4) Part II of the application

27. The following statements are about types of information systems that insurance companies use. Select the answer choice that contains the correct statement.

    (1) A transaction processing system can produce documents that provide information to the recipient, but it cannot produce documents that request an action from the recipient.
    (2) A decision support system (DSS) is a system of hardware and software designed to analyze information and actually recommend or make specific decisions.
    (3) An expert system is a group of computer programs that organizes data in a database, allows users to obtain the information they need, and controls how databases are structured, accessed, and maintained.
    (4) A transaction processing system is designed to perform high-volume, routine, and repetitive business exchanges, such as application processing, policy issue and administration, premium billing, claim administration, and salary and commission payment.

28. One phase in the product development process for an insurance product is the technical design phase. During the technical design phase of life insurance product development, an insurer

    (1) conducts concept testing to measure the acceptability of new product ideas
    (2) evaluates new product ideas quickly and inexpensively and identifies those ideas that warrant further investigation
    (3) obtains necessary regulatory approvals of policy forms from each jurisdiction in which the insurer intends to issue and sell the product
    (4) creates the contract provisions and language, pricing and benefit structures, producer compensation structures, and issue and underwriting specifications for the new product

29. A bond rating is a letter grade assigned by a bond rating agency to indicate the credit quality of a bond issue. With regard to the meanings of bond ratings, it is generally correct to say that, the higher the bond rating, the

    (1) safer the bond investment
    (2) higher the default risk of the bond
    (3) more likely the bond is to be a high-yield bond
    (4) higher the expected rate of return of the bond

30. An insurer sometimes measures its profitability using the return on capital ratio. With regard to the return on capital ratio, it is correct to say

    (1) that the return on capital ratio can be calculated only for the insurer as a whole, rather than for a line of business or a specific product
    (2) that the return on capital ratio can be unweighted or it can be weighted to take into account the insurer's level of risk
    (3) that the information needed to calculate the return on capital ratio is found only on the insurer's balance sheet
    (4) that, the higher the return on capital ratio, the *less* effectively the insurer has used its resources to generate a profit during a given period

31. A financial statement is a report that summarizes a company's financial situation or major monetary events and transactions. The financial statement that lists the values of a company's assets, liabilities, and capital and surplus as of a specific date is known as

    (1) a balance sheet
    (2) an income statement
    (3) a statement of operations
    (4) a statement of owners' equity

32. Insurers purchase new issues of securities through public offerings and private placements, and they purchase or sell previously issued securities on securities exchanges and through over-the-counter (OTC) markets. With regard to these methods of buying and selling securities, it is correct to say

    (1) that, in a public offering, the issuing firm must register the security with the appropriate government agency, such as the Securities and Exchange Commission (SEC) in the United States
    (2) that public offerings have become a preferred way for insurers and other institutional investors to purchase new issues of securities
    (3) that issuing securities as private placements takes more time and is more costly than making a public offering
    (4) that an OTC market is a market in which buyers and sellers of securities (or their agents or brokers) meet in one location to buy and sell securities

33. A business or government that issues a bond is legally obligated to pay the bondholder a specified amount of money on a specified date, known as the maturity date. The amount of money owed on the maturity date is specified on the bond and is known as the bond's

    (1) call provision
    (2) coupon rate
    (3) collateral
    (4) face value

34. There are seven principles that guide insurers and regulators in their attempts to protect consumer privacy. Some of these principles relate to accountability, transfer, access, and data integrity. With regard to these privacy principles, it is correct to say that the principle of

    (1) *accountability* refers to allowing a customer the right to review and correct his personal information
    (2) *transfer* refers to how a company adheres to the principles of notice and consent when transmitting data to third parties
    (3) *access* refers to providing a customer with information about when, how, and to whom his nonpublic personal information will be disclosed
    (4) *data integrity* refers to the physical, technical, and procedural measures a company takes to prevent the loss, wrongful disclosure, or theft of customers' personal information

35. During group life insurance underwriting, insurers consider many risk assessment factors, including the size of the group, the age and sex distribution of group members, and the stability of the group. With respect to these risk assessment factors, it is generally correct to say

   (1) that, in comparison to small groups, large groups tend to have more and larger fluctuations in claims
   (2) that, in comparison to small groups, large groups generate less administrative expense as a percentage of the total premium amount the group pays
   (3) that, for groups of all sizes, underwriters consider the age and sex of each individual group member
   (4) that a group whose membership remains unchanged over a long period of time presents a lower risk in comparison to a group that has a steady flow of new, younger members entering the group as current members age and eventually leave the group

36. An underwriter found that a proposed insured's anticipated mortality is higher than average because the proposed insured recently had heart surgery. Although the proposed insured presents a higher-than-average mortality risk, the underwriter considers the proposed insured to be insurable. In classifying the risk that the proposed insured presents to the insurer, the underwriter most likely would assign the proposed insured to the

   (1) preferred class
   (2) standard class
   (3) substandard class
   (4) declined class

37. When Evan Ryland called the Hampton Insurance Company for information about his annuity, a computer-based technology answered the telephone call, greeted Mr. Ryland with a recorded message, and prompted him to enter his account number using the telephone keypad.
   Mr. Ryland selected the option to be transferred to a customer service representative (CSR). Hampton's automated telephone system used Mr. Ryland's account number to search a database for his customer profile. The system then forwarded the customer profile to a CSR's computer so that the profile appeared on the CSR's computer screen at the same time Mr. Ryland's call was connected to the CSR. From the following answer choices, select the response that correctly indicates the type of computer telephony integration (CTI) that answered Mr. Ryland's telephone call and the type of CTI that allowed Hampton's system to deliver voice and data simultaneously to a CSR's workstation.

	CTI that answered Mr. Ryland's call	CTI that delivered call and data to CSR
(1)	an automated workflow system	screen pop
(2)	an automated workflow system	electronic data interchange (EDI)
(3)	an interactive voice response (IVR) system	screen pop
(4)	an interactive voice response (IVR) system	electronic data interchange (EDI)

38. The Sutton Insurance Company is based in a European country that belongs to a trade organization whose goal is to unify member European countries into a single market of goods, services, investments, and people. Because Sutton's home country is a member of this organization, Sutton is allowed to operate in other member countries. The trade organization issues insurance directives to improve the consistency of insurance regulation and facilitate competition among its member countries. This information indicates that Sutton's home country is a member of the organization known, by definition, as the

   (1) European Union (EU)
   (2) World Trade Organization (WTO)
   (3) Organization for Economic Cooperation and Development (OECD)
   (4) International Association of Insurance Supervisors (IAIS)

39. An underwriter at a United States life insurance company evaluated the following third-party life insurance applications to ensure that each applicant had an insurable interest in the life of the proposed insured:

   • Anjali Brown applied for a policy insuring the life of her business partner, May Leong
   • Thomas Renfro applied for a policy insuring the life of his grandmother, Violet

   It is correct to say that the underwriter most likely found insurable interest to exist in

   (1) both Ms. Brown's and Mr. Renfro's applications
   (2) Ms. Brown's application only
   (3) Mr. Renfro's application only
   (4) neither Ms. Brown's nor Mr. Renfro's applications

40. Functional areas in an insurance company are sometimes classified as line units or staff units. An example of a *staff* unit in an insurance company is the

   (1) actuarial department
   (2) underwriting department
   (3) compliance department
   (4) annuity administration department

41. Section 1035 of the United States Internal Revenue Code permits the tax-free exchange of specified types of insurance and annuity policies. The following statements describe requests for policy replacements. Select the answer choice that correctly describes an exchange that does **NOT** qualify as a permissible Section 1035 exchange.

   (1) Alvin Daley wants to replace his life insurance policy with an annuity policy.
   (2) Zoey Serrano owns a life insurance policy insuring only her life, and she wants to replace the policy with a life insurance policy that insures both her life and her husband's life.
   (3) Nuala Corrigan owns an annuity policy where annuity benefits are payable to her, and she wants to replace the policy with another annuity policy where annuity benefits are payable to her.
   (4) Grant Ewing owns a life insurance policy insuring only his life, and he wants to replace the policy with another life insurance policy that insures only his life.

42. Astrid Swensen is the beneficiary of a $250,000 whole life insurance policy insuring the life of her mother, Inga Swensen. Inga died while the policy was still in force, and Astrid filed a claim for the policy proceeds. A claim analyst used the following information about the policy to calculate the benefit amount:

- Outstanding policy loan = $2,500
- Accrued policy loan interest = $125
- Accumulated policy dividends = $300
- Premiums due and unpaid = $500
- Paid-up additional coverage that Inga purchased = $5,000

This information indicates that the total benefit amount payable to Astrid is

(1) $246,575
(2) $252,075
(3) $252,175
(4) $252,425

43. The organization chart at the Wexton Insurance Company shows the structure of authority that flows downward from the higher levels of the organization to the lower levels. This information indicates that Wexton's organization chart shows the company's

(1) chain of command
(2) functional regulation
(3) controlling interests
(4) corporate charter

44. An Annual Statement is a document that presents information about an insurer's operations and financial performance, with an emphasis on demonstrating the insurer's solvency. With regard to the Annual Statement, it is correct to say that every life insurer operating in the United States is required to file its Annual Statement with the

(1) National Association of Insurance Commissioners (NAIC) only
(2) Securities and Exchange Commission (SEC) and the NAIC
(3) NAIC and the insurance department of every state in which the company conducts business
(4) SEC and the insurance department of every state in which the company conducts business

45. The Montclair Insurance Company maintains several required reserves and contingency reserves in addition to policy reserves. One of these reserves is designed to absorb gains and losses in Montclair's investment portfolio. By definition, this type of reserve is known as an

(1) asset valuation reserve, which is a type of contingency reserve
(2) asset valuation reserve, which is not a type of contingency reserve
(3) asset fluctuation reserve, which is a type of contingency reserve
(4) asset fluctuation reserve, which is not a type of contingency reserve

46. Michael Portnoy, an insurance producer, sold a whole life insurance policy with an annual premium of $1,500, and the policy remained in force for eight years. The insurer used the following commission schedule to compensate Mr. Portnoy: a first-year commission rate of 55%, a vested renewal commission rate of 4% for five years after the first policy year, and a typical service fee of 1% of the premium. Mr. Portnoy serviced the policy for the entire eight years, during which time the policy's annual premium stayed the same. This information indicates that the total amount of compensation most likely paid to Mr. Portnoy on this policy was

    (1) $1,140
    (2) $1,155
    (3) $1,245
    (4) $1,275

47. In accounting, the process of classifying items in a financial transaction as assets, liabilities, capital and surplus, revenue, or expenses, and recording the transaction in a company's accounting records, is known as

    (1) recognition
    (2) auditing
    (3) budgeting
    (4) activity-based costing (ABC)

48. The following statements describe security measures that two companies use to protect information as it travels over a network:

    • To protect data traveling over a network from unauthorized access, the Kensington Life Insurance Company uses technology that encodes data so that only an authorized person possessing the required hardware and software can decode the data.
    • The Concord Financial Assurance Company has a secure computer network that uses a combination of hardware and software to act as a "tunnel" through the Internet so that only people in possession of the required technology have access to data traveling through the network.

    With respect to types of security measures for information systems, this information indicates that Kensington is using a security measure known as

    (1) encryption, and Concord is using a security measure known as a firewall
    (2) encryption, and Concord is using a security measure known as a virtual private network (VPN)
    (3) intrusion detection software, and Concord is using a security measure known as a firewall
    (4) intrusion detection software, and Concord is using a security measure known as a virtual private network (VPN)

49. The Plymouth Life and Health Insurance Company maintains a management information system (MIS) that provides Plymouth managers with various types of reports. While conducting a research project, a manager requested from the MIS a special report on the policy lapse rates in a specified geographic area. This type of MIS report is best described as

    (1) an ad hoc report
    (2) an exception report
    (3) a scheduled report
    (4) an edit report

50. One typical investment objective of an insurer is to maintain an adequate spread. With regard to an insurer's investment policy, spread is defined correctly as the

    (1) excess of investment income over investment expenses
    (2) amount by which an investment's selling price exceeds its purchase price
    (3) return earned on an investment during a given time period expressed as a percentage of the purchase price
    (4) difference between the rate of return earned on the insurer's investments and the interest rate credited on its products

51. Some insurance companies develop comprehensive customer profiles as part of their customer relationship management (CRM) programs. One type of information found in a comprehensive customer profile is customer *wallet share*, which is best defined as

    (1) the economic benefit of the relationship with a customer calculated over time
    (2) the customer's current level of satisfaction with a company and its service
    (3) all insurance policies, annuities, and other financial products that the customer has purchased from the insurance company or financial institutions that are affiliated with the company
    (4) the percentage of a customer's business on a particular type of product that the customer places with a company

52. Underwriters in the United States and Canada often request information about proposed insureds from MIB Group, Inc. (MIB). With regard to MIB information, it is correct to say that

    (1) MIB allows its member companies to use MIB information as the sole basis for an unfavorable underwriting decision
    (2) MIB members may request additional information about impairments that applicants have disclosed, but they may not request information about impairments that applicants did not disclose on their current applications for insurance
    (3) MIB requires an insurer to obtain a proposed insured's written consent to obtain and use the information for underwriting evaluation before the insurer requests the information from MIB
    (4) insurers obtain information from MIB, but they do not report information about proposed insureds to MIB

53. Marketing analysts in life insurance companies gather information about factors in the external marketing environment. Two categories of external environmental factors that concern an insurer are the economic environment in which the insurer operates and the social environment that consists of customer groups. With regard to changes in the economic environment and the social environment, it is generally correct to say

    (1) that high or rising stock prices tend to decrease the public's demand for variable and equity-based insurance products
    (2) that high inflation tends to decrease the level of interest rates
    (3) that, in many countries, the median age of the population is rising due to increasing birth rates and decreasing life expectancies
    (4) that the proportion of single-parent family households and the proportion of nonfamily households have increased in many countries

54. In some jurisdictions, a mutual insurer has the option of converting to a mutual holding company. The following statements are about mutual holding company conversions. Select the answer choice that contains the correct statement.

    (1) A mutual holding company conversion requires the approval of only the mutual insurer's board of directors and its policyowners.
    (2) The timing of the initial public offering (IPO) is less flexible under a mutual holding company conversion than under demutualization.
    (3) If a mutual insurer redomesticates to a state that permits mutual holding companies, the insurer is not required to meet the incorporation requirements of the state that will be its new domiciliary state.
    (4) A newly formed mutual holding company is generally required to maintain at least a 51 percent interest in its intermediate stock holding company, and the intermediate stock holding company must control 100 percent of the newly formed stock insurance subsidiary.

55. Insurers use several types of mortality tables, which are charts that show the projected death rates among a particular group at each age. Common types of mortality tables include basic mortality tables, valuation mortality tables, annuity mortality tables, life insurance mortality tables, and unisex mortality tables. With regard to these types of mortality tables, it is generally correct to say that

    (1) basic mortality tables are less conservative than valuation mortality tables
    (2) basic mortality tables have a safety margin built into the mortality rates
    (3) annuity mortality tables usually project higher rates of mortality than do life insurance mortality tables
    (4) unisex mortality tables reflect the fact that, as a group, women experience lower mortality at all ages than do men

56. To determine the loading charge for an insurance product, actuaries must make assumptions about the amount of operating expenses related to the product. Insurers typically classify operating costs into four categories: development expenses, acquisition expenses, maintenance expenses, and overhead expenses. *Acquisition* expenses include the costs of

   (1) preparing new policies and new customer records
   (2) planning and creating insurance products
   (3) disbursing policy benefits
   (4) conducting research and general actuarial analysis

57. Some insurance companies are organized by organizational units known as strategic business units (SBUs). One typical characteristic of an SBU is that the unit

   (1) is responsible for its own costs and revenues
   (2) relies on its parent company to conduct strategic planning for the unit
   (3) produces a product or service that faces no outside competition
   (4) eliminates the duplication of effort, particularly among support functions, that can occur in a company that is organized more traditionally

58. Underwriters at some insurance companies consult pharmaceutical databases during the underwriting process. With respect to the organizations that maintain these databases and to the type of information contained in these databases, pharmaceutical databases are typically maintained by

   (1) insurers, and this type of database contains the results of laboratory tests, such as blood chemistry profiles, that an insurer has ordered for underwriting
   (2) external vendors, and this type of database contains an organized collection of information about the medications that have been prescribed for individuals in the general population
   (3) physicians, and this type of database contains information about a proposed insured's medical conditions and treatments
   (4) consumer reporting agencies, and this type of database contains information about a proposed insured's health and personal life

59. The Dahlia Life Insurance Company, a stock insurer, acquired the Wellington Financial Company and the Hunley Company. Dahlia Life then created Lexford Holdings to own Dahlia Life, Wellington Financial, and the Hunley Company. With regard to the holding company arrangement described in this situation and the control of the companies involved, it is correct to say that Lexford is

   (1) an upstream holding company, and Dahlia Life controls Wellington Financial, the Hunley Company, and Lexford Holdings
   (2) an upstream holding company, and Lexford Holdings controls Dahlia Life, Wellington Financial, and the Hunley Company
   (3) a downstream holding company, and Dahlia Life controls Wellington Financial, the Hunley Company, and Lexford Holdings
   (4) a downstream holding company, and Lexford Holdings controls Dahlia Life, Wellington Financial, and the Hunley Company

60. The following statements are about market conduct examinations conducted by state insurance departments in the United States. Select the answer choice that contains the correct statement.

    (1) The insurance department in each state is required by law to conduct periodic, on-site investigations of insurance companies operating within that state.
    (2) The purpose of a market conduct examination is to identify and monitor threats to an insurer's solvency.
    (3) A state insurance department has the authority to fine an insurer that is found to have violated state insurance laws or regulatory requirements, but does not have the authority to suspend or revoke the insurer's license to conduct business in that state.
    (4) A state insurance department is prohibited from conducting a target examination of an insurer more frequently than every three years.

61. In the United States, one important federal privacy law that affects life insurance underwriting regulates the reporting and use of consumer credit information and seeks to ensure that reports from consumer reporting agencies contain only accurate, relevant, and recent information. This federal privacy law is known as the

    (1) Insurance Information and Privacy Protection Model Act
    (2) Unfair Trade Practices Act
    (3) Fair Credit Reporting Act (FCRA)
    (4) Privacy of Consumer Financial and Health Information Regulation

62. An actuary at the Laurel Life Insurance Company is calculating the cost of benefits for a life insurance product for a group of insureds ages 75 and 76. He is using the following partial mortality table that shows the projected mortality rates for this group of life insureds:

Age	Mortality per 1,000	Number living	Number dying
75	12.00	250,000	3,000
76	12.96	?	3,200

From the following answer choices, select the response that correctly identifies the total number of insureds living at age 76 and whether, as the mortality rate increases for the group of insureds from age 75 to age 76, Laurel's cost of benefits increases or decreases.

	Number living at age 76	Effect of the mortality rate increase
(1)	246,800	The cost of benefits increases
(2)	246,800	The cost of benefits decreases
(3)	247,000	The cost of benefits increases
(4)	247,000	The cost of benefits decreases

63. Omar Mahmoud, a supervisor, evaluated the job performance of Henry Song. The following excerpt is from the form that Mr. Mahmoud used to rate Mr. Song on the performance factor of leadership:

Performance Factor	Rating = 5	Rating = 4	Rating = 3	Rating = 2	Rating = 1
Leadership: Influences others toward quality and productivity	Consistently inspires others toward greater achievement	Frequently takes the role of leader	Sometimes acts as group leader	Rarely takes the lead on team projects or solves problems	Avoids taking on a leadership role or new responsibility

This information indicates that Mr. Mahmoud rated Mr. Song's job-related characteristics using a performance evaluation method called

(1) the ranking method
(2) a critical incident evaluation
(3) management by objectives (MBO)
(4) a behaviorally anchored rating scale (BARS)

64. Two insurance companies in the United States incorporated in the following manner:

- The Field Life Insurance Company incorporated in State A and does business in State A and State B
- The Stream Life Insurance Company incorporated in State B and does business in State B and State A

From the answer choices below, select the response that correctly identifies, from the viewpoint of *State A*, the type of insurer that Field Life and Stream Life represent.

	Field Life	Stream Life
(1)	domestic insurer	foreign insurer
(2)	domestic insurer	alien insurer
(3)	resident insurer	domestic insurer
(4)	resident insurer	foreign insurer

65. A claim analyst at the Riverglen Life Insurance Company received a claim for the proceeds of a life insurance policy still in its contestable period. In investigating the claim, the claim analyst discovered a material misrepresentation on the application for the policy. As a result of this discovery, Riverglen began a legal proceeding under which it sought to have the insurance contract declared void from the beginning because of the material misrepresentation. This information indicates that Riverglen underwent a legal process known as

(1) policy filing
(2) mediation
(3) rescission
(4) interpleader

66. The Canterbury Insurance Company distributes its insurance products through commissioned salespeople who hold agency contracts with several insurance companies. These salespeople work alone, are not housed in any insurer's field office, and engage primarily in personal production. They spend most of their time selling insurance and annuities rather than building and managing an agency. This information indicates that Canterbury uses the nonagency-building distribution system that is known as the

    (1) personal-producing general agency system
    (2) location-selling distribution system
    (3) brokerage distribution system
    (4) multiple-line agency distribution system

67. During the comprehensive business analysis phase of product development, employees in many functional areas are involved in researching certain technical and operational aspects of a new product. One functional area reviews the proposed product to determine the financial reporting requirements the insurer must meet in developing and selling the product. This area also evaluates how the business will be reflected in the company's financial statements. The functional area that most likely handles these tasks is the

    (1) investments area
    (2) accounting area
    (3) agency operations area
    (4) actuarial area

68. For the purposes of Annual Statement reporting, life insurers in the United States divide their assets into three categories: admitted assets, nonadmitted assets, and partially admitted assets. From the following answer choices, select the response that correctly identifies an example of a typical admitted asset and an example of a typical nonadmitted asset.

Admitted asset	Nonadmitted asset
(1) computer equipment	account receivable due in less than 90 days
(2) account receivable due in less than 90 days	cash
(3) cash	furniture
(4) furniture	speculative securities

69. Statistical studies have identified factors associated with differences in mortality. The following statements are about the effect of these factors on general mortality patterns. Select the answer choice that contains the correct statement.

    (1) Married individuals usually experience higher mortality than do unmarried individuals.
    (2) Lower-than-average income and education are typically associated with lower-than-average mortality.
    (3) Workers covered under employee group insurance tend to experience higher mortality than does the general population.
    (4) Hourly-paid employees generally experience higher mortality than do salaried employees.

70. The following statements are about various types of agency-building distribution systems. Select the answer choice that contains the correct statement.

   (1) Like most other agents, home service agents are allowed to accept initial premiums for a life insurance policy, but not renewal premiums for the policy.
   (2) Insurance companies often use the salaried sales distribution system for selling group insurance products through group representatives.
   (3) In a branch office system, the branch manager typically pays all the business and operating expenses that the branch office incurs.
   (4) In the general agency system, an insurer pays the salaries of a general agency's support staff and most or all of the operating expenses of the agency office.

71. The Walden Life Insurance Company is a small insurer with limited resources. Walden uses a target marketing strategy that focuses all of its marketing resources on offering credit life insurance to new credit card users. This focus has allowed Walden to compete with larger insurers in the credit life insurance business and has allowed Walden to gain extensive expertise in the credit life business. This information indicates that Walden uses a target marketing strategy known as

   (1) mass marketing
   (2) concentrated marketing
   (3) differentiated marketing
   (4) undifferentiated marketing

72. Companies in all industries are exposed to various types of general business risk. One risk that a life insurance company faces is *strategic risk*, which is the risk that the company

   (1) will experience financial loss as a result of deficiencies in company systems, business processes, personnel, or internal controls
   (2) will not implement appropriate business plans and strategies needed to adapt to changes in its business environment
   (3) will be unable to obtain necessary funds to meet its financial obligations on time without incurring unacceptable losses
   (4) will set the premium rates on a product either too low to generate enough revenue to cover the product's claims and other expenses or too high to compete with similar products

73. After a product is in force and an insurance company accumulates experience with it, the insurer looks at any deviations between the actual values from experience and the assumed values used in pricing. A situation in which an *adverse deviation* arises occurs when

    (1) actual benefit payments are lower than assumed
    (2) actual company expenses are lower than assumed
    (3) actual company revenue is higher than assumed
    (4) actual policy lapse rates are higher than assumed

74. During the product development process, insurers generally establish product design objectives as part of a comprehensive business analysis. Product design objectives for an insurance product typically specify

    (1) the product's financial requirements, potential unit sales, revenues, costs, and profits
    (2) the product's basic characteristics (such as benefits), the manner in which the benefits will be provided, applicable fees and charges, and any limitations on issuing policies
    (3) all the environmental factors that might affect sales of the product, including the nature and size of the product's target market and the potential appeal of the product to customers
    (4) the marketing goals and strategies for the product, including detailed activities involving the pricing, promotion, and distribution for the product

75. After Boris Markov resigned from his position at the Blanca Financial Services Company, Blanca's human resources (HR) manager conducted an interview to discuss Mr. Markov's opinions about working conditions at Blanca and ways of improving any problem areas. The HR manager holds these meetings with most employees who leave the company to gather information about employee grievances and current or potential problems in the workplace. The meeting that the HR manager conducted with Mr. Markov can best be described as

    (1) a screening interview
    (2) an exit interview
    (3) a discharge interview
    (4) outplacement counseling

END OF EXAMINATION

Answer choice explanations are available on the CD-ROM on the inside back cover of this book.

Text References
and Answers to
Sample Examination

Text References and Answers to Sample Examination

Interactive Study Aid Software Instructions

Running the Interactive Study Aid Software

The minimum recommended PC configuration for the Interactive Study Aid is as follows:

- A Pentium or better PC
- Microsoft Windows 95

The Interactive Study Aid (ISA) is located on the TPG Companion CD-ROM on the inside back cover of this book. The ISA runs directly from the CD. Therefore, you do not need to install the ISA on your computer's hard drive. The ISA will typically auto-start when you insert the CD into your computer's CD-ROM or DVD-ROM drive. If it does not auto-start, click the Windows Start button, choose Run, and enter x:\isa.exe, substituting your CD-ROM's drive letter (typically d: or e:) for x:.

If the CD-ROM contains only the Interactive Study Aid, the study aid's Startup Screen will appear first. If the CD-ROM contains more than the Interactive Study Aid, the first screen to pop up will allow you to select which program or file you want to access on the CD.

If you have difficulty running the software, you can obtain technical support from LOMA's Help Desk at 770-984-3782 from 8 a.m. to 5 p.m. Eastern Time.

The Help Desk should be contacted only for technical support regarding problems in operating the software. Other comments, including comments about the content of the sample exam, should be sent to:

LOMA
Examinations Department
2300 Windy Ridge Pkwy, Suite 600
Atlanta, GA 30339

or faxed to the Examinations Department at 770-984-3742, or e-mailed to education@loma.org.

Overview of the Interactive Study Aid

In this section, we give you an overview of how the Interactive Study Aid works.

Sample Examination, Case Studies, and Practice Questions. The ISA includes a Sample Examination, as well as chapter-by-chapter Case Studies and Practice Questions. The Case Studies are available on the ISA only. The Sample Exam and Practice Questions are the same as the ones included in the printed manual that accompanies the ISA, but the ISA includes answer choice explanations not found in the printed manual. The answer choice explanations provide you with immediate feedback on why your selected answer choice is correct or incorrect.

Let's run through the steps involved in using the software:

Startup Screen

The first screen that appears when you launch the ISA allows you to tell the software which course you want to study from. The courses are packaged into .ISA files, such as *Study Aid for LOMA 286.isa*. Follow the instructions on the first screen to select your .ISA file, then click the **Next >** button.

Main Menu

The Main Menu appears after the Startup Screen. At the Main Menu, you select whether to study from the Sample Exam, a chapter's Case Studies, or a chapter's Practice Questions. You can also click the **Restart** button on the Main Menu to restart a previously saved study session.

The Main Menu also contains information about the textual materials upon which the course's examination items were based. The first step you should take is to look up the course's current text assignment and ensure that the textbook(s) listed in the software match the current assignment. You should double-check the edition numbers and copyright dates of the textbooks. We want you to be sure that you are studying from the correct textbooks, and with the correct, up-to-date .ISA course file.

You can look up the current course assignment in the LOMA Education and Training Catalog, which is free and available via download from www.loma.org (click on the Downloads button). If you determine that the ISA you are using is based on an out-of-date text assignment, see your Ed Rep to obtain an up-to-date study aid manual for the course. The current ISA CD will be included at the back of that manual.

At the Main Menu, you have the following options:

- **Case Studies.** Several Case Studies are included for each chapter. These Case Studies are designed to help you learn the material as you read through the text. When you choose the Case Studies option, you also need to select the textbook and chapter from which to study.

- **Practice Questions.** These are chapter-by-chapter practice questions that allow you to test your knowledge of each chapter. When you choose the Practice Questions option, you also need to select the textbook and chapter from which to study.

■ **Sample Examination.** This is a full examination similar in content and difficulty level to the actual examination you will sit for.

■ **View Answer Choice Feedback.** If this option is enabled, then answer choice explanations are available to you. The answer choice explanations will pop up in the answer choice explanation display.

Typically, you would want to check this option, so that you get the full benefit of the ISA. One situation in which you might not want to view the feedback is as a sort of simulation of the actual test-taking experience. Taking the Sample Exam without benefit of the explanations allows you to test your knowledge of the material and preparedness for the real exam.

The ISA also provides you with additional feedback in the form of a green checkmark and a red X. The checkmark indicates a correct answer, and the X indicates an incorrect answer. These graphics appear next to your selected answer choice. This feedback always appears in the Case Studies and Practice Questions, and appears in the Sample Exam if you choose to view the answer choice feedback.

Select the options you want, then click the **Go** > button to continue to the question display.

Question Display

Once you move from the Main Menu into the examination itself, you'll be presented with the question display window. This window displays the current examination question.

Recording your answer. To record your answer to a question, click the round "radio" button immediately to the left of your chosen answer choice, or press the corresponding number key on the computer's keyboard. The question display also contains five toolbar buttons at the top left of the display. Four of these buttons are used for navigating through the examination and are always visible; the fifth is visible when you complete all of the Sample Exam questions or all of a chapter's Case Studies or Practice Questions, and is used to go to the score report.

As long as "Button Help" on the "Options" menu is checked, a help "balloon" will appear below a button when you move the mouse cursor over the button. The balloon gives you a brief explanation of what the button does. Click the Button Help menu option to toggle the button help on and off.

Here is a brief explanation of each of the toolbar buttons:

 Return to the previous question

 Go to the next question

 Choose the number of a question to jump to. You can also jump to a question by clicking the question's number in the question list at the left side of the question display.

Go to the first remaining unanswered question. Clicking this button causes the software to scan through the exam questions in sequence, to determine the first question for which you have not yet submitted an answer. The program will then take you to that question.

 This button appears only after you complete all of the Sample Exam's questions or all of the current chapter's Case Studies or Practice Questions. Click this button (or choose Get Score Report from the Options menu) to go to the score report.

If you return to a question that you've already answered, the "radio" button of the answer you chose will be selected. Typically, the selected radio button will correspond to the first answer choice you selected, because your "grade" on the Sample Exam or a chapter's Practice Questions is based on your first choice when you're receiving answer choice feedback.

This "first-response" grade allows you to judge how well you did on the exam questions without the benefit of the answer choice feedback. Since you'd typically want to keep selecting answer choices until you get the question correct, if the ISA graded your last response, your grade would be 100% every time, instead of being a more accurate reading of how well you knew the material going into the question.

The only exception to the first-response grade is if you choose to take the Sample Exam without viewing the answer choice explanations. Since you do not get the benefit of any answer choice feedback in this situation, the ISA will record your final response.

You can customize the font and font size of the question display panel by selecting **Preferences** from the **Options** menu.

Exam Status. You can get a quick view of how you are doing on the examination by going to the **Options** menu and selecting **Exam Status**. A window will appear that indicates the answers you've selected thus far.

Saving a Session. If you have to interrupt a study session in the software, but want to be able to resume the session later, you can save your progress to a file by choosing **Save** from the **File** menu. In the SaveAs dialog box that appears, choose the drive and/or directory where you want to save the file, enter a name in the "File Name" box, and click the OK button. The software will save the pertinent information it needs to be able to restore your session at a later time.

To resume the session, click the **Restart** button on the Main Menu. In the File Open dialog box that appears, select the drive and directory where you stored the file (it will have a .TST extension), click on the file name, and then click the OK button. The ISA will read in the data from the file and will resume the session where you left off.

Exiting the Exam. To quit the study session at any time, select **Exit to Main Menu** from the **File** menu. Once at the Main Menu, if you want to exit the Interactive Study Aid, click on the Main Menu's **Exit** button.

Completing the Last Question. When you have answered all of the Sample Exam's questions or all of the current chapter's Case Studies or Practice Questions, a message will pop up informing you of that fact. To get your score report after viewing that message, either select **Get Score Report** from the **Options** menu, or click the 'checkmark' button that gets added to the end of the toolbar.

Score Report

This report indicates the number of questions you answered correctly. The score report for a chapter's Case Studies or Practice Questions will show your score on that chapter. The score report for the Sample Exam shows your overall score, and provides you with a chapter-by-chapter grade summary. This chapter-by-chapter summary will show you how well you did on the questions from each chapter. This information will help you to identify those chapters on which you need to focus your additional studies. At an absolute minimum, you should devote some extra study time to those chapters for which your score was less than 70%.

Note that you can view the full chapter-by-chapter grade report ONLY if you complete all of the exam questions.

There are three buttons on the grade report.

Click the **Review the questions I missed** button to return to the study session and rework the questions that you missed. In reviewing the questions you missed, you'll automatically be presented with the answer choice explanations (if such explanations are available), regardless of whether or not you chose the option on the Main Menu to view the explanations. Once you've completed the review, the software will offer you the opportunity to review the questions you missed on the preceding review. You can keep cycling through these reviews of missed questions until you answer all the questions correctly on the first try. You can exit the review at any time by selecting **Exit to Main Menu** from the **File** menu.

Click the **Print my grade report** button to send a copy of your grade report to the printer. A print options dialog box will appear. Select the applicable options for your printer and select OK.

Click the **Exit to the main menu** button to return to the main menu.

For more complete information on using the Interactive Study Aid, see the software's online help file (choose Contents from the Question Display screen's Help menu).

TPG COMPANION CD LICENSE AGREEMENT